Essential Histories

The Crimean War

Essential Histories

The Crimean War

John Sweetman

OSPREY
PUBLISHING

First published in Great Britain in 2001 by Osprey Publishing,
Elms Court, Chapel Way, Botley, Oxford OX2 9LP
E-mail: info@ospreypublishing.com

ISBN 1 84176 186 9

Editor: Rebecca Cullen
Design: Ken Vail Graphic Design, Cambridge, UK
Picture research carried out by Image Select International
Cartography by The Map Studio
Index by Alan Rutter
Origination by Grasmere Digital Imaging, Leeds, UK
Printed and bound in China by L. Rex Printing Company Ltd

01 02 03 04 05   10 9 8 7 6 5 4 3 2 1

For a complete list of titles available from Osprey Publishing
please contact:

Osprey Direct UK, P.O. Box 140,
Wellingborough, Northants NN8 4ZA, UK
E-mail: info@ospreydirect.co.uk

Osprey Direct USA, P.O. Box 130,
Sterling Heights, MI 48311-0130, USA
E-mail: info@ospreydirectusa.com

Or visit our website:
www.ospreypublishing.com

Contents

Chronology

1853 **28 February** Menshikov mission arrives Constantinople
21 May Menshikov leaves Constantinople
8 June British fleet leaves Malta for eastern Mediterranean
2 July Russian troops cross Pruth river to invade Moldavia and Wallachia
14 October British and French fleets anchor in the Dardanelles
23 October Turkey declares war on Russia
30 November 'Massacre' at Sinope; Turkish flotilla sunk
24 December Sir James Graham (First Lord of the Admiralty) calls for destruction of Sevastopol

1854 **3 January** British and French fleets enter Black Sea
11 January Russia warned that warships in Black Sea must return to Sevastopol
13 February Cabinet approves Lord Raglan's appointment as C-in-C, British Expeditionary Force
22 February First troops leave England
27 February Russia must undertake within six days to withdraw from Moldavia and Wallachia by end of April
11 March Baltic fleet leaves Portsmouth
26 March First French troops leave for Turkey
27 March France declares war on Russia
28 March Britain declares war on Russia
30 March Vanguard of British Expeditionary Force at Malta ordered to Gallipoli
8 April British troops at Gallipoli; French already there

10 April Britain and France sign treaty of alliance; Raglan leaves London
15 April Turkey formally joins the allies
22 April Naval bombardment of Odessa
29 April Raglan reaches Constantinople
7 May St Arnaud lands at Gallipoli
11 May Siege of Silistria starts
23 May Britain, France, Austria and Prussia guarantee Turkish independence
25 May French troops sail for Varna
29 May British troops sail for Varna
22 June British naval squadron blockades the White Sea
23 June Siege of Silistria raised
2 July Russians recross Pruth river, vacating Moldavia and Wallachia
16 July Raglan receives Cabinet dispatch requiring invasion of the Crimea
18 July Allied Council of War to discuss invasion
21 July Mouth of Katcha river chosen as landing area
10 August Serious fire in Varna delays invasion; cholera also prevalent
24 August Embarkation commences; bad weather further disrupts timetable
31 August Anglo-French naval squadron attacks Petropavlosk
5 September Raglan reaches Balchik Bay; French commander (St Arnaud) already gone
9 September Raglan carries out another reconnaissance of Crimean coast; chooses Calamita Bay for landings
13 September Eupatoria surrenders
14 September Allied landings commence in Calamita Bay; last until 18 September

19 September Advance on Sevastopol commences; skirmish at the Bulganek river

20 September Battle of the Alma

23 September Southward advance resumes; Russian warships sunk to block Sevastopol harbour entrance

25 September Flank march commences; Canrobert succeeds St Arnaud as French C-in-C

27 September Siege of Sevastopol begins

29 September St Arnaud dies of cholera at sea

2 October British naval brigade lands

13 October Patriotic Fund founded for wives and orphans of servicemen lost in the Crimea

17 October First Bombardment of Sevastopol

25 October Battle of Balaclava

26 October Skirmish of Little Inkerman

4 November Florence Nightingale reaches Scutari

5 November Battle of Inkerman

6 November Allied Council of War decides to continue siege

14 November The Great Storm

1855 2 January Sardinia joins allies

5 January Omar Pasha lands in the Crimea with Turkish reinforcements

25 January J. A. Roebuck's resolution, critical of the conduct of the war, leads to resignation of Lord Aberdeen's government

5 February Lord Palmerston Prime Minister

17 February Russian attack on Eupatoria

24 February More Russian ships sunk at Sevastopol

2 March Death of Nicholas I; succeeded by Alexander II

5 March Sevastopol Select Committee commences work

4 April Second Baltic fleet leaves England

9 April Second Bombardment of Sevastopol

3 May Abortive first expedition sails for Kertch

22 May Kertch expedition relaunched

6 June Third Bombardment of Sevastopol

7 June Capture of the Quarries and the Mamelon

11 June White Sea again blockaded

13 June French troops leave Kertch

14 June British troops leave Kertch, Turkish garrison remains

17 June Fourth Bombardment of Sevastopol

18 June Failed attacks on the Great Redan and Malakov; report of Sevastopol Committee to Parliament

28 June Death of Lord Raglan; succeeded by Sir James Simpson

16 August Battle of the Tchernaya

17 August Fifth Bombardment of Sevastopol

5 September Sixth Bombardment of Sevastopol

6 September Omar Pasha leaves Crimea

8 September French capture Malakov; British fail at the Great Redan

9 September Allies occupy southern Sevastopol

7 October Combined force sails for the Dnieper river

17 October Capture of Kinburn on the Dnieper

11 November Sir William Codrington succeeds Simpson as British C-in-C

15 November Ammunition explosion in French lines

25 November Surrender of Kars

16 December Austrian peace plan submitted to St Petersburg

1856 16 January Tsar accepts peace terms

29 January Last major Russian bombardment across Sevastopol Bay from the north

28 February Armistice signed in Paris

29 February Opposing officers meet amicably in Crimea

30 March Treaty of Paris signed

27 April Treaty of Paris ratified

12 July Last British troops leave Crimea

Panorama of the conflict

In 1783 Catherine the Great annexed the Crimea, prefacing a series of military ventures around the shores of the Black Sea to further Russia's territorial ambitions. Seventy years on, another violent episode was about to begin. On 27 March 1854, the British Parliament was informed that 'Her Majesty feels bound to afford active assistance to her ally the Sultan against unprovoked aggression.' Next day, *The London Gazette* contained the declaration of a war that would not formally end until 27 April 1856. During the intervening 25 months, Britain combined with Turkey, France and Sardinia against Russia as both sides courted Austria and Prussia, which were hovering on the sidelines.

Three allies. (L to R) Lord Raglan, Omar Pasha and General (later Marshal) Pélissier, commanders of the British, Turkish and French land forces in the Crimea, 7 June 1855. General de la Marmora led the Sardinian contingent. (Hulton Getty)

Scope of fighting

Many streets, rows of terraced dwellings, official buildings, even children (girls christened Alma) would be triumphantly named after the victories of British soldiers, their first commander and acclaimed heroes during the Crimean War. The signs of many public houses to this day proudly display 'Battle of Inkerman', 'Sevastopol Arms', 'The Lord Raglan', 'Cardigan of Balaclava'. The Charge of the Light Brigade remains a stirring example of selfless devotion to duty and military discipline, the subject of three feature films and innumerable articles, books and television programmes.

This lingering impression of unalloyed celebration masks the realities of a costly, debilitating conflict, whose shortcomings were highlighted at the time and have been eagerly gnawed by ravenous critics ever since. With the Russian fleet bottled up in its principal Black Sea port, a combined British, French and Turkish force landed in the Crimea just south of Eupatoria, 30 miles (48km) north of its target, Sevastopol. The plan for a swift *coup de main* went badly wrong, and the invaders were condemned to besieging their quarry from exposed upland to the south during biting winter conditions, as the ranks of men and horses were decimated by disease and starvation. A long campaign under such privation not having been anticipated, the supply, transport and medical arrangements woefully broke down. Before peace settled over the hills, valleys and shattered remains of Sevastopol, approximately 22,000 British, a minimum 80,000 French, possibly 10,000 Turks, 2,000 Sardinians and more than 100,000 Russians had perished.

However, this was a war with Russia, not merely one of her small, southern peninsulas. Contemporaries referred to the 'Russian War'; soon after its conclusion E. H. Nolan and W. Tyrell respectively published two- and three-volume histories of 'The War with Russia'. It was not quite a worldwide struggle, but the vast territories of the enemy dictated far-flung operations. So, Petropavlovsk in the Pacific, the Kola peninsula and shores of the White Sea in the Arctic were attacked. British support went to the Turks on the Danube and the unsuccessful defence of Kars in Asia Minor.

Major Anglo-French expeditions were sent into the Baltic in 1854 and 1855 (a third was

Baltic fleet at Spithead, 1854. A powerful British fleet left Spithead in March 1854, being joined in the Baltic four months later by a French flotilla carrying troops. It returned to England in November. (Hulton Getty)

planned for 1856) to discourage Russian warships at Kronstadt from venturing into the North Sea and perhaps to entice Sweden into the allied camp. Both were dispatched with great pomp. On 11 March 1854, Vice-Admiral Sir Charles Napier's fleet, led by the 131-gun *Duke of Wellington*, was cheered away from Spithead by waving thousands on shore and the Queen in the royal yacht *Fairy*. Alfred Lord Tennyson reputedly penned part of his poem *Maud* after seeing this grand example of maritime power: 'It is better to fight for the good than to rail at the ill.' Napier's 18 ships with 1,160 guns would later be joined by 23 French warships with 1,250 guns and troops under Vice-Admiral P. Deschenes to capture shore installations in a formidable allied armada.

Rear-Admiral Sir Richard Dundas sailed on 4 April 1855 with a second expedition,

comprising lines of battleships and frigates supported by floating batteries, mortar vessels and gunboats, Napier's having returned home before the onset of winter. Dundas' warships were all screw, none purely sail; but there were no troops this time with the French squadron, which joined them on 1 June. 'Bomarsund' and 'Sveaborg' would appear on memorial obelisks, as mute recognition of successful actions carried out during the two Baltic forays.

In truth, though, action beyond the Black Sea has claimed little lasting attention. To posterity, the battles in the Crimea – the Alma, Balaclava, Inkerman, Sevastopol, the Tchernaya – are infinitely more recognisable. What happened between the allies and Russia between 1854 and 1856 is more

Sevastopol. Looking east, with strong fortifications covering the harbour entrance, naval dockyard middle right and old lighthouse in the distance. The northern suburb is left, across Sevastopol Bay. (Author's collection)

readily identified with military activity on and around the south-western corner of that peninsula than anywhere else. 'The Crimean War', not 'The War with Russia', has become firmly established in historical legend.

Furthermore, obsessive concentration by commentators on publicised disasters overlooks the multitude of colourful firework displays, flamboyant military reviews, musical celebrations and municipal banquets that heralded the signing of peace. Citizens of Britain, France, Turkey and Sardinia rejoiced at defeating Russia. Households

Vice-Admiral Sir Charles Napier (1786–1860). Commander of the British Baltic fleet in 1854, which lacked spectacular success and was replaced for the 1855 expedition. (Hulton Getty)

mourned the loss of loved ones, but family correspondence and the wording on war memorials showed pride that their sacrifice had preserved national honour and overcome evil. In Britain, this embodied the spirit of the mid-Victorian age.

Press influence

What made this a different kind of conflict was that the public and politicians at home quickly learnt its graphic details. Extension of an electric telegraph cable right up to the allied positions before Sevastopol and its regular use by newspaper reporters on the spot made this possible. W. H. Russell of *The Times* was the most famous, but not the only, 'war correspondent' in the Crimea: representatives of several other journals and newspapers filed reports for domestic consumption. The sheer novelty of the process added enormously to its impact, akin to the impact of television

William Howard Russell (1820–1907). *The Times'* correspondent in the Crimea, whose reports shaped public and political opinion in Britain and contributed to the fall of Lord Aberdeen's government in February 1855. (Hulton Deutsch)

news bulletins in the late twentieth century. Eyewitnesses, especially civilians not associated with the military machine, acquired an aura of authority and measured judgement. Their bias and the validity of their information were not closely questioned. Stories straight from the front were presumed to be accurate and authentic.

Clamour for action in editorials during the first quarter of 1854 had built up a public head of steam for war. Exposure of perceived shortcomings at the front undermined the reputations of individuals like the British commander Lord Raglan, highlighted inconsistencies in the archaic structure of military administration, brought down a government at Westminster and created a favourable climate of opinion for fundamental change in the organisation of the army. Successive Cabinet ministers, politically responsible for the conduct of the war, used press reports to criticise Raglan and his staff. Lord Panmure declared, for

example, that 'your staff must be changed, at least that will satisfy the public and that radically ... I must do something to satisfy the House of Commons'. Members of Parliament gained their information almost exclusively from newspapers and periodicals; Panmure's predecessor, the Duke of Newcastle, made clear that official reports from the front were sparse and inadequate.

Photographers, too, added a new dimension to warfare, the most celebrated but by no means the sole practitioner in the Crimea being Roger Fenton. Their impact, though, was more retrospective, less immediate.

Divided command

Unfortunately, civilian reporters were unschooled in the byzantine nature of military administration, and thus blamed Raglan and his staff officers for matters over which they had no effective control. At the outset of the war, the artillery and engineers were responsible directly to the Master-General of the Ordnance, not the Commander-in-Chief at the Horse Guards,

Roger Fenton (1819–69). One of several photographers working in the Crimea and there for only four months in 1855, Fenton produced a series of impressive images of life at the front. (Hulton Getty)

who controlled the infantry and cavalry. Two legally distinct British armies therefore existed. The Royal Navy was, of course, an entirely separate entity as well, answerable to the Lords of the Admiralty in Whitehall and to nobody in the Crimea. So Raglan could only request, not demand, co-operation from the naval commander off-shore in the bombardment of Sevastopol and the provision of sea transport to the Turkish mainland for the sick and wounded. The civilian Ordnance Department supplied military equipment, while the Commissariat (a Treasury department) looked after food and land transport; Raglan relied on them without commanding them. The entire ramshackle structure palpably lacked co-ordination.

Moreover, unlike the Duke of Wellington as allied Commander-in-Chief in the Peninsular War, Raglan had no authority over the other national forces. The Turkish, French and Sardinian contingents had their own commanders, all independent of one another. The press, public and politicians never fully appreciated the constraints that this put on drawing up strategic plans or executing tactical operations against defence

works like the Redan and Malakov in the ring of Sevastopol's fortifications.

Turkey or Russia?

One fundamental question persists. Was the death of approximately one-fifth of army personnel sent to the Crimea, exclusive of naval and civilian casualties, the acute disruption of domestic life and the prolonged misery of the wounded and bereaved ultimately worthwhile? In 1856 the British, French, Turkish and Sardinians celebrated victory. Yet, within 15 years, Russia had unilaterally abrogated the main provisions of the peace treaty. Looking back and aware that the Turkish Empire in south-eastern Europe had soon disintegrated in a welter of damaging international conflicts, Lord Salisbury mused that Britain ought to have sided with Russia, not Turkey. He could not know that in the Balkans the seeds of the First World War were already germinating. If the Crimean War had not been fought, would this European catastrophe have been avoided?

Opposing forces

In March 1854, for Britain to declare war on Russia in support of Turkey appeared both wise and necessary. The underlying reasons were long term, part of the so-called Eastern Question – the disintegration of the Turkish Empire, which stretched from the Alps to Egypt. Russia, and in particular her Black Sea fleet, represented a menacing unknown quantity in this equation, the Tsar in repeated conversations with the British ambassador describing Turkey as ripe for rich picking, 'the sick man of Europe'. For the past 200 years Russia had been spreading territorial tentacles outwards from Moscow, southwards into the Ukraine and in 1783 to the Crimea. There Sevastopol provided a warm-water port from which the fleet could sail through the Bosphorus and Dardanelles Straits into the eastern Mediterranean, directly to threaten British trade routes with the Levant and India.

Overland probes in the Caucasus west of the Caspian Sea underlined Russian desire for even further expansion into the Near East. But these advances were too distant to perturb Europe. Incursions across the Danube into the Balkans towards Constantinople, occupation of which would allow Russian warships their free passage into the Mediterranean, were altogether a different matter. Only international diplomatic pressure had halted Russian troops uncomfortably close to the Turkish capital in 1829. An even more serious crisis evolved in 1833. With Asia Minor threatened by the advance of rebel forces into Syria under Ibrahim, son of the pasha of Egypt, Mehemet Ali, the Sultan turned to Russia for help: 'A drowning man will clutch at a

serpent,' his foreign minister observed. Nicholas I's price for moral and diplomatic support, without firing a shot or in any way actively intervening, was Turkish agreement to close the Straits to foreign warships on Russia's request.

Not for nine years could Britain engineer the expulsion of the Egyptians from Syria and fashion a new agreement whereby the Straits would be closed to all warships in time of peace. Russia's exclusive influence had therefore been removed, but this incident re-emphasised the Tsar's designs on the Straits. Despite his comments about Turkey's pseudo-medical condition, in 1844 Nicholas I protested to Prince Albert that 'he did not want an inch of Turkish territory'. Palmerston thought this 'a great humbug … one is denying the teaching of history if one believes that Russia is not thinking of extending to the south'.

Nicholas I (1796–1855). Succeeded Alexander I as Tsar of Russia in 1826. Reputedly died of a broken heart on 2 March 1855 following Russian failure to recapture Eupatoria. (Ann Ronan Picture Library)

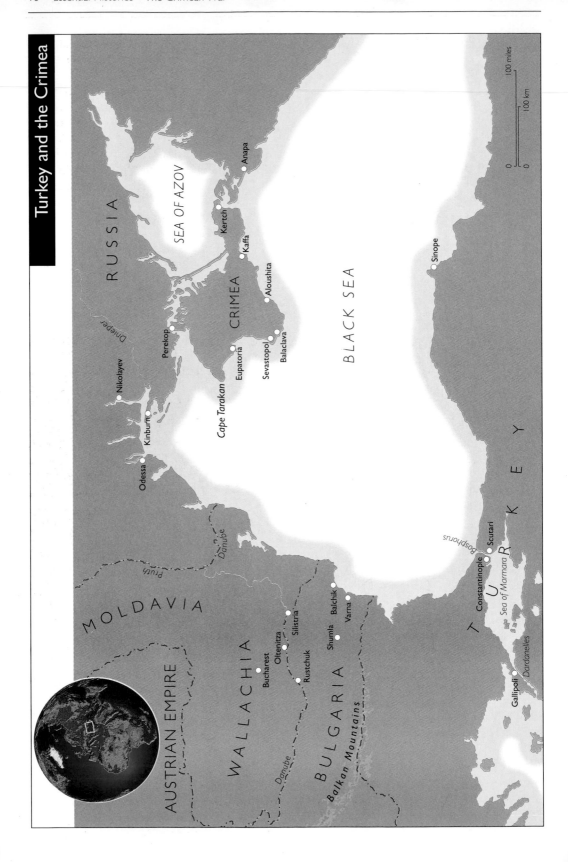

Turkey and the Crimea

RUSSIA

SEA OF AZOV

Anapa

Kertch

Kaffa

CRIMEA

Aloushita

Perekop

Dnieper

Eupatoria

Sevastopol

Balaclava

Cape Tarakan

BLACK SEA

Sinope

Nikolayev

Kinburn

Odessa

MOLDAVIA

Danube

Pruth

Bosphorus

Scutari

Constantinople

Sea of Marmara

T U R K E Y

Balchik

Varna

Silistria

Shumla

Oltenitza

Bucharest

Rustchuk

WALLACHIA

Danube

BULGARIA

Balkan Mountains

AUSTRIAN EMPIRE

Dardanelles

Gallipoli

100 miles

100 km

Disputed areas

Most of the Sultan's subjects in south-eastern Europe, between the Black Sea and the Adriatic, were Christian. Alleged ill treatment of them by the Turks, whose military and political might was now quite visibly crumbling, provided a ready excuse for external intervention. Aware of Russian aspirations, other European powers needed to be vigilant. The Tsar, however, counted on lethargy among his potential opponents, whose co-operation, seen to effect in 1829 and 1841, might one day fail through inertia or preoccupation with more pressing problems.

As another diplomatic crisis developed in 1852, this seemed likely. Nicholas I looked for neutrality at the very least from Prussia and Austria, both of which had benefited from his help to crush internal liberal revolutions between 1848 and 1851. France had acute troubles at home, having deposed her king in 1848, and experienced the *coup d'état* three years later that made Louis Napoleon into Emperor Napoleon III. Britain, the Tsar calculated, was isolated. He had not counted on the strength of commercial self-interest – in Britain's case, protection of the Indian trade routes; in France's, the opportunity for further markets and financial investment in Turkey. Furthermore, a diplomatic or military triumph over Russia would enhance the new French Emperor's credentials both nationally and internationally.

Unresolved disputes in 1852 and 1853 between Catholic monks (backed by France) and Orthodox monks (supported by Russia) over guardianship of holy places in Jerusalem, then part of the Turkish Empire, were the occasion, not the cause, of the Crimean War. Underlying tensions of long-standing origin were fundamentally responsible. The Tsar refused to accept Turkish attempts at compromise and dispatched a mission to the Porte with demands for recognition of Russia's guardianship over the whole of Turkey's 14 million Christian subjects. To Prince A. S. Menshikov, who led this mission,

Nicholas wrote: 'if Turkey did not yield, then the ambassador extraordinary [Menshikov] must threaten the destruction of Constantinople and the occupation of the Dardanelles'. Meanwhile, Nicholas I was proposing a partition of European Turkey between Britain, Austria and Russia, with France taking Crete. Reputedly, only firm rejection from Field Marshal I. F. Paskevich stopped the Tsar from using the Black Sea fleet to force the Straits and land troops on the shores of the Bosphorus. So much for no territorial claim.

Prompted by Britain and France, the Sultan rejected Menshikov's demands, and on 8 June 1853 the British Mediterranean fleet at Malta was ordered to 'the

Napoleon III (1808–73). As Louis Napoleon, exiled in London before becoming President of the Second French Republic in 1848. Three years later, after a *coup d'état*, proclaimed Emperor. Keen to gain international prestige and recognition in the Crimean War, in 1855 he briefly planned to take command personally in the field. (Ann Ronan Picture Library)

neighbourhood of the Dardanelles ... for the protection of Turkey against an unprovoked attack and in defence of her independence'. On 2 July, scarcely a month after departure of the abortive mission from Constantinople, Russian troops crossed the Pruth river to enter Moldavia and Wallachia (modern Romania, then two provinces under Turkish suzerainty). Their orders were to obtain 'by force, but without war ... [Russia's] just demands ... [as] various arbitrary acts of the Porte have infringed the rights [of Christians]'. Russia was going 'to the defence of the Orthodox religion'.

Allied deliberations

Representatives of the major European nations met to determine what they should do. As a deterrent, Austria moved forces to her south-eastern border. But after Russia ignored an ultimatum to leave the Turkish provinces, on 23 October Turkey declared war. At this point, no intervention by Britain seemed necessary, for the Turks had 100,000 men along the Danube blocking the way south. They soon gave a good account of themselves. Crossing the river, the Sultan's troops occupied fortified positions on the north bank, and during the opening days of November they drove off determined Russian assaults on Oltenitza.

The situation changed dramatically on 30 November. A weak Turkish squadron was surprised in Sinope harbour on the southern coast of the Black Sea, 350 miles (560km) east of Constantinople, by a strong Russian flotilla including six ships of the line, two frigates and four steamers. The Russians took advantage of poor visibility to destroy the Turkish ships with a reported loss of 4,000 men. A lone steamer escaped to carry the news to Constantinople, whence two British warships set off to render belated aid. Harrowing reports of struggling swimmers raked by Russian cannon, as they left their stricken vessels, provoked massive pro-Turkish public demonstrations in Britain. It emerged that the Russians had used

explosive shells, a lethal invention that was somehow deemed underhand and unfair. Moreover, the Turkish admiral had apparently been lulled into a false sense of security, because Russia had announced that her immediate interests were confined to the Danubian provinces.

The press dubbed what had happened 'a foul outrage ... a massacre'. In London, the *Morning Advertiser* accused Britain and France of interfering diplomatically only 'to betray unfortunate Turkey'. Members of the British government, it claimed, were 'imbecile men, the minions of Russia', adding: 'Has Justice ceased to occupy her throne in the English heart? Has the national honour lost its hold on the people of this realm?' The *Westminster Review* drew attention to 'our passage to India', informing its readers that 'our merchants will rue the blind folly in declining to stop him [the Tsar]'. *The Times* proclaimed that 'an aggressive posture was not only moral, Christian and patriotic, but self-evidently judicious, businesslike and manly' – a potent combination of sentiments. *Punch* published a cartoon of the Prime Minister, Lord Aberdeen, blacking the Tsar's boots. *The Spectator* referred to 'war with the most powerful and unscrupulous state in Europe, or peace on degrading terms'.

Drift to war

Lord Palmerston, the Home Secretary, represented a broad swathe of opinion in declaring that 'something must be done to wipe away the stain [of Sinope]', seen in twenty-first-century terms as a crime against humanity. Thus, on 3 January 1854, British and French naval squadrons entered the Black Sea with Turkish connivance. Eight days later a formal note to St Petersburg demanded that all Russian warships return to Sevastopol, warning too that any further naval aggression against Turkey would be met by force. On 27 February, Britain required that within six days Russia undertake to withdraw from the two provinces by the end of April: 'Refusal or silence ... [would] be

Henry John Temple, Lord Palmerston (1784–1865). Home Secretary in 1854, Palmerston was keen to confront Russia. Benefiting from public dissatisfaction at failure to take Sevastopol, he became Prime Minister in February 1855. (Ann Ronan Picture Library)

equivalent to a declaration of war.' The Tsar did not reply. Even before the formal declaration of war on 28 March, British troops had begun to leave south-coast ports amid scenes of wild enthusiasm, and British and French officers were in Turkey to inspect the defences of Constantinople and plan for allied intervention.

Prospects for a peaceful solution had not yet altogether gone. British, French, Prussian and Austrian representatives were still in diplomatic conclave, Napoleon wrote personally to Nicholas I, and a Quaker delegation went from London to St Petersburg. Aberdeen optimistically, though futilely, held that 'I, for one, deny … that war is inevitable.' But the British and French declarations came almost simultaneously, and on 10 April the two countries signed a treaty of alliance (acceded to five days later by Turkey). Next day, the Tsar in turn declared war on Britain and France, protesting that 'Russia fights not for the things of this world, but for the Faith'. Commenting on British enthusiasm for war, Charles Greville (Clerk to the Privy Council) prophetically wrote in his diary: 'Before many months are over, people will be heartily sick of it, as they are now hot upon it.' Years later, the pacifist John Bright observed: 'When people are inflamed in that way, they are no better than "mad dogs".'

In the House of Commons, John Ball reflected majority opinion inside and outside of Parliament in speaking of the need to fight 'for the maintenance in civilised society of the principles of right and justice'. This was a just war. Unfortunately, the Tsar thought so as well.

A just war

Three months before Britain went to war, on 24 December 1853 Sir James Graham (First Lord of the Admiralty) focused attention on the Crimea. He argued that command of the Black Sea, which would preserve the integrity of Turkey and deny Russian warships passage through the Straits, could be secured only by 'the entire destruction of Sebastopol [*sic*] with its naval and military establishments'. But the known strength of the port's massive seaward fortifications, which protected the entrance to the harbour, ruled out a successful naval attack without the assistance of a land force. Graham and the Duke of Newcastle (Secretary of State for War and the Colonies) therefore began to visualise such a combined operation with Sevastopol as the prize. In the wake of public and political reaction to the Sinope affair, events moved ahead speedily.

Britain

On 7 February, the Master-General of the Ordnance, Lieutenant-General Lord Raglan (soon promoted general and, before the end of the year, field marshal) was verbally offered the post of 'General Officer Commanding the Forces eastwards of Malta'. Six days later the Cabinet approved his appointment. Some reservations were expressed about his age (65) and lack of campaign experience after the Battle of Waterloo in 1815. Since 1819 he had held a series of high-ranking staff appointments but, in truth, he had never commanded in the field. However, he had served at the Duke of Wellington's side, first as his aide-de-camp (ADC) then as Military Secretary from 1808 to 1815, and he had been on the staff of the British Embassy in Paris from 1814 to 1818, besides leading a

FitzRoy Henry James Somerset, Field Marshal Lord Raglan (1788–1855). Aged 65, Raglan accepted command of the British Expeditionary Force to Turkey, and ultimately the Crimea, as a matter of duty. Having no authority over his fellow French, Turkish and Sardinian commanders and exercising limited control even over British support services, he was nevertheless blamed for shortcomings in the field. He died of dysentery and exhaustion in the Crimea, 28 June 1855. (Hulton Deutsch)

diplomatic mission to Spain in 1823. He accompanied Wellington to the Congress of Verona (1822) and to St Petersburg (1825) for the coronation of Nicholas I, whose troops he was set to fight.

In his lengthy career, Raglan had proved himself adept at dealing with difficult men

Lieutenant-General Sir George Brown (1790–1865).
Commanded the 1st Infantry Division in the
Crimean Expeditionary Force. Fought bravely at
the Alma and Inkerman, where he was seriously
wounded. Led the allied expedition, which captured
Kertch in May 1855, but was invalided home
shortly afterwards. (Ann Ronan Picture Library)

and delicate situations, such as threats to
public order in London during presentation
of the third Chartist petition to Parliament
in 1848. He was not only familiar with
France, but also fluent in the French
language. This made him an ideal choice for
dealing with a touchy ally. His tact would be
fully extended in dealing with three
successive French commanders and a proud
Turkish Commander-in-Chief (C-in-C),
sensitive to any perceived slight. Diplomacy,
as much as military acumen, would be
required for the forthcoming campaign.

Initially, on 8 February, the Cabinet agreed
to dispatch 10,000 troops to Malta, although
Newcastle acknowledged that more would be
needed if 'a trial of strength' with Russia were
to develop. By mid-March, Britain, France
and Turkey were informally looking to
national contingents of 5,000 with which to
invade the Crimea. Raglan chose his own
immediate staff (adjutant-general,
quartermaster-general and military secretary)
and ADCs, but he could only recommend
officers to command divisions and brigades.
He did not always get his way. The Cabinet
would not approve Sir George Brown as his
second-in-command, and Raglan's protests at
putting the volatile lords Lucan and Cardigan
in close proximity were overridden.

Urbane, thoughtful and courteous, Raglan
inspired fierce loyalty in those close to him.
But he disliked ostentation – invaluable for a
commander in projecting himself to a wider
spectrum of his own troops and those of his
allies. A thoroughly decent man who
accepted command of the Expeditionary
Force as a matter of patriotic duty, he was
loath to exert his authority, preferring an
appeal to reason.

Lieutenant-General Sir George Brown (64)
took charge of the Light Division. A strict
disciplinarian, he had fought in the

Peninsular War and since 1815 he had held a
series of senior staff appointments, including
that of Adjutant-General at the Horse
Guards. He had quarrelled, however,
with Wellington's successor as C-in-C
(Lord Hardinge) and resigned.

Lieutenant-General the Duke of
Cambridge, the Queen's 35-year-old cousin
who had never seen action, commanded the
1st Division of infantry after royal pressure
for his appointment. He had served in
the Hanoverian Army, briefly led the
17th Lancers during the Chartist troubles,
then held administrative posts in Corfu and
Ireland. Lieutenant-General Sir George de
Lacy Evans (67) had the 2nd Division. With
experience, like Brown and Raglan, in the
Peninsular War, he had also served in India
and with the British Legion during the
Carlist Wars in Spain. But his radical politics
and tendency to fall out with senior officers
had stunted his career.

Major-General Sir Richard England (61),
commanding the 3rd Division, had fought in
India and the Kaffir Wars in southern Africa.
The 4th Division went to Major-General the
Hon. Sir George Cathcart (60), another war
veteran from southern Africa. An added
complication was that, Brown having been

Lieutenant-General George Frederick Charles, Duke of Cambridge (1819–1904). Queen Victoria's cousin, commander of the 1st Infantry Division. Fought at the battles of the Alma and Inkerman; played a peripheral part in the Battle of Balaclava. Invalided home in November 1854. (Ann Ronan Picture Library)

commanders, only Lucan had battle experience. Curiously, that had been when attached to the staff of the Russian force that crossed the Danube into the Balkans in 1828–29, with some sources placing him in command of a cavalry formation in the latter stages of that campaign.

Two field artillery batteries with 6pdr or 9pdr guns were attached to each infantry division, except the Light, which had one field battery and one troop of horse artillery. The Cavalry Division had one troop of horse artillery with it. Heavier guns (up to 32pdrs) were allocated for siege purposes, enhanced before Sevastopol by naval 68pdrs and revolutionary, rifled Lancaster guns. The experienced Royal Engineer Lieutenant-General Sir John Fox Burgoyne (71) would join Raglan's staff in an advisory capacity before the Crimean landings. Excluding the Heavy Brigade, which did not land with the main body, officially 26,095 men of all ranks invaded the Crimea under Raglan's command, supported by 60 guns.

The British fleet in the Black Sea, comprising 16 warships with a total of 645 guns, was commanded by Vice-Admiral Sir James Dundas, with Rear-Admiral Sir Edmund Lyons in command of its in-shore squadron. Once it became clear that the Russian navy had been blockaded in Sevastopol, a Royal Navy brigade went ashore with guns from several ships to swell the besieging force.

France

Marshal St Arnaud (52), who had seen active service in Algeria and supported Louis Napoleon during his coup d'état in 1851, led the French Expeditionary Force. Brown thought him 'a strange, flighty fellow and one it will not do to take at his word'; years later Christopher Hibbert declared him 'brave, gay, unscrupulous and resourceful'. His force consisted of four divisions, each of two brigades with three regiments, commanded by generals F. C. Canrobert (45), P. J. F. Bosquet (44), Prince Napoleon-Jérôme

vetoed as Raglan's deputy, Cathcart received a 'dormant commission' by which he would assume command should Raglan be incapacitated; but that was not widely known.

Each of the five infantry divisions comprised two brigades of three battalions, making a total of about 4,000 men per division. The Light and 4th divisions contained an additional rifle battalion.

The Cavalry Division was under Major-General (soon local Lieutenant-General) Lord Lucan (54), its Heavy Brigade being led by Brigadier-General the Hon. James Scarlett (55) and the Light Brigade by Lucan's brother-in-law, Major-General Lord Cardigan (57). Each brigade comprised five regiments totalling 1,000 sabres. Of the three cavalry (the Emperor's cousin, 32) and E. F. Forey (49). When the French landed in the Crimea, St Arnaud had 25,000 infantry, 2,800 other troops (some sources put the combined total at 30,200) and 68 guns, but no cavalry. Thus the only cavalry available to the allied commanders in the first phase of the invasion was the British Light Brigade.

Under the separate command of Vice-Admiral F. A. Hamelin, though subject to greater control by the land force commander than his British counterpart, the French fleet initially comprised 12 battleships and steamers (totalling 780 guns), increasing to 25 warships before the landings in the Crimea.

General Omar Pasha (1806–71). As Turkish C-in-C in the Balkans, he fiercely resisted Russian besiegers of Silistria in 1854. Established a close working relationship with Lord Raglan. After the fall of Sevastopol, led a relief column that failed to save Kars. (Ann Ronan Picture Library)

Turkey

The Turks landed 7,000 infantry and attached them to the French for the march south. Their C-in-C, Omar Pasha, remained at Shumla with a large force in reach of the Danube, deeply suspicious that a renewed advance into the Balkans might take place once the allies had been committed to the Crimea. Eventually, some 30,000–35,000 Turks would serve on the Crimean peninsula, mainly in defence of Eupatoria or in the siege lines before Sevastopol. Omar Pasha spoke French, German and Italian, though heavily accented, and his background was extraordinary. Formerly a Croat named Michael Lattas, he had left the Austrian for the Turkish army, converted to Islam, then acquired a new name and a fierce reputation fighting anti-Turkish rebels in the Balkans. The Turks had 11 sail and steam ships under their own admiral in the Black Sea.

Marshal Armand Jacques Leroy de St Arnaud (1801–54). After supporting Napoleon III's *coup d'état*, St Arnaud was appointed C-in-C of the French Expeditionary Force in 1854. Unsuccessfully attempted to secure overall command of the English force and to dominate allied strategy. Surrendered command to Canrobert on 25 September; died four days later. (Ann Ronan Picture Library)

Russia

Aware of the problems associated with a divided allied command, Bosquet remarked: 'The Russians have one enormous advantage over us: their army has only one chief.' That was an illusion. The Crimean peninsula had two Russian commanders-in-chief: in the west, Prince A. S. Menshikov; for eastern Crimea and north-west Caucasus, General P. F. Khomutov, who controlled 12,000 men and the supply route into Sevastopol from the Sea of Azov via Kertch and Theodosia.

Menshikov had no authority over Khomutov and, although his command included the Black Sea Fleet as well as land forces, several more junior officers had effective autonomy beneath him. Vice-

Admiral V. A. Kornilov, chief of staff to the Black Sea fleet and an excellent organiser, commanded the garrison of Sevastopol with his subordinate naval commander, Vice-Admiral P. F. Nachimov (victor at Sinope, senior to Kornilov but reluctant to take the garrison post). Lieutenant-General F. F. von Moeller, Menshikov's most experienced divisional commander, acted in a similar

General Prince Alexander Sergeevich Menshikov (1781–1869). Nominally C-in-C, Western Crimea, but effectively commander of the forces resisting the allied invasion, he lost the Battle of the Alma through poor deployment of troops in a strong defensive position. After establishing a field army on the flank of allied troops besieging Sevastopol, he failed to use it effectively. Dismissed after the abortive Russian attack on Eupatoria in February 1855. (Ann Ronan Picture Library)

capacity for the army. Lieutenant-Colonel F. E. I. Todleben, a 37-year-old engineer, was in charge of making the port's land fortifications effective.

An accomplished linguist and well read, Prince A. S. Menshikov had wide civil and military experience. He had served in the Napoleonic Wars, been seconded to the Foreign Ministry, held naval rank and appointments including Chief of the Naval Staff, been Minister for the Navy and Governor-General of Finland. The year before Britain and France declared war, the diplomat General B. D. A. de Castelbajac referred to Menshikov's 'simple and polished manners', love of 'women, gambling, horses, good and bad company … witty and caustic repartee'. Menshikov's disdainful treatment of the Sultan during his mission to Constantinople in 1854, which Nicholas I's physician believed 'simply furnished him with a fresh excuse for witticisms and jokes', underlined his aristocratic demeanour and intolerance of those he considered inferior. Critics held that he rarely, if ever, consulted others, although he was careful to cultivate the Tsar. A Russian academic, Professor Tarle, has concluded that Menshikov viewed all appointments as his due. Flexibility of outlook and self-criticism were anathema to him. They were qualities much needed in the months ahead.

When the allies landed on 14 September 1854, excluding Khomutov's command and units still in transit from Bessarabia and mainland Russia, Menshikov had 38,000 soldiers and 18,000 seamen at his disposal. The previous day, 600 Congreve rockets had arrived to enhance his artillery capability. When 11 French foragers were captured on 15 September and revealed that the allied force exceeded 50,000, Menshikov asked Khomutov for another Cossack cavalry regiment, the Moskov infantry regiment and an additional field battery.

Until now, he had suspected that the landings near Eupatoria were a feint to draw troops away from Sevastopol and lay it open to a *coup de main*. Not including 5,000 civilian workmen, the total of strength of the Sevastopol garrison once the siege developed was later known to be 30,850 – a mixture of militia battalions, one regular battalion of infantry, artillery and marine personnel, supplemented by seamen from warships withdrawn into harbour from the Black Sea. However, when the allies landed near Eupatoria estimates of the number of Russian troops on the Crimean peninsula varied wildly. For the Russians, work rapidly took place to strengthen the defences of Sevastopol, and within a fortnight of the invasion 172 guns (many of them heavier than those of the besiegers) were in place to combat an assault from the southern upland. Eastwards across the Tchernaya, at the end of September Menshikov had a field army of approximately 30,000 men (including regiments withdrawn from Sevastopol), which would be further reinforced via the Perekop peninsula in the north and Sea of Azov to the east.

The numbers on both the allied and Russian sides would vary greatly during the forthcoming hostilities, due to battle casualties, disease and reinforcements. But when the allies invaded on 14 September 1854, the forces facing one another on the peninsula were each about 60,000 men.

The clash of arms

After a farewell audience with the Queen, Lord Raglan left London by train for Dover on 10 April 1854. Arriving in Paris the following morning, during the ensuing week he had discussions with St Arnaud, other senior officers and Napoleon III. Leaving the French capital on 18 April, travelling via Marseille, Malta and Gallipoli, he reached Constantinople 11 days later.

Meanwhile, British warships had 'opened the ball with Russia'. Seeking to evacuate the British and French consuls from Odessa, *Furious* had been fired on by shore batteries, and naval reinforcements were summoned to avenge this outrage. A ten-hour bombardment on 22 April devastated Odessa's military installations and caused 1,100 casualties. However, five British ships were also damaged. Battle had been joined.

On land, during February Sir John Burgoyne and the French engineer Colonel Ardent had begun inspecting the defences of Constantinople, as other officers surveyed Turkish positions on the Danube. The first British troops left Southampton on 22 February and frequent departures occurred thereafter from that port, Portsmouth, Plymouth and Liverpool. Large crowds waved away the early departures, but by the time the 8th Hussars left Plymouth on 25 April the fuss had died down. Stopping only briefly at Gibraltar, the early troopships berthed at Malta for troops to enjoy the mild climate and cheap wine. At this stage, peace might yet prevail. On 30 March, however, orders were issued to proceed to Gallipoli under Sir George Brown, pending Raglan's arrival.

Landing on 8 April, the British found that their French allies had preceded them and laid claim to the best accommodation and food. By the end of May, some 18,000 British and 22,000 French were in the vicinity.

Several British units moved further north to Scutari, where conditions were scarcely better. It was with considerable relief therefore that in June, apart from a small garrison at Gallipoli and a transit depot at Scutari, troops were ordered to Bulgaria through the port of Varna. Once more, though, Britain's ally beat them to the best billets and supplies.

French troops at Gallipoli. The first location occupied by allied forces and soon overcrowded. By June 1854, it retained only a small garrison as the bulk of the units moved on. (Ann Ronan Picture Library)

Grenadier Guards leave London. A contemporary print showing the Grenadiers marching to Waterloo Station, cheered by an enthusiastic crowd of men, women and children. (Author's collection)

Bulgarian summer

In the early summer of 1854, the Russians were still occupying Moldavia and Wallachia and threatening Turkish positions along the Danube, especially the fortress of Silistria on its southern bank. If this fell and enemy troops poured into the Balkans, the allies would need to bolster the Turks in Bulgaria; hence the advance to Varna. But before Raglan left England, Newcastle had instructed him that, although his 'first duty' was to protect Constantinople, if the enemy made no 'onward movement it may become

Silistria. Fortress south of the Danube, besieged by Russian forces in 1854. Fears that it would fall resulted in allied troops moving into Bulgaria. The Russians withdrew on 23 June, leaving the allies free to invade the Crimea. (Ann Ronan Picture Library)

essential for the attainment of the objects of the war that some operations of an official character should be undertaken by the Allied armies ... No blow ... struck at the southern extremities of the Russian Empire would be so effective for this purpose as the taking of Sebastopol [sic].'

So the prospect of an allied invasion of the Crimea was always in Raglan's mind. However, it would not be easy to organise. St Arnaud, in command of the larger French force, tried to gain control of the two armies and to dictate their deployment in Bulgaria. Only firm action by Raglan, including a personal appeal to the Sultan with detailed reference to the tripartite agreement guaranteeing independent, national commands, avoided major confrontation. However, Raglan quickly established a good working relationship based on mutual respect with Omar Pasha, whom he visited at his headquarters in Shumla.

The neighbourhood of Varna rapidly became overcrowded, and the British moved further inland to the valleys of Devna and Aladyn. There cholera struck in addition to debilitating dysentery and fevers. Relocation of the camps did not noticeably stem the flow of fatalities: during July, 600 died in a fortnight. Serious deficiencies in the hospital services, which relied heavily on recalled military pensioners gathered into an optimistic Hospital Conveyance or Ambulance Corps, were cruelly revealed. So were supply problems. Some troops still carried the smooth-bore Brown Bess musket, instead of the new Minié rifled version; on 15 June, Raglan complained that the 3rd Division lacked 1,300 promised Miniés.

Ten days later, Raglan informed Newcastle of a deficiency that would never be satisfactorily solved during the entire campaign: 'The means of [land] transport form our principal want and a most serious one.' Under a system named 'waggons of the country', carts and drivers would be recruited on contract in the area of operations. This proved totally unrealistic in Bulgaria, and later in hostile Crimea. Regular provision of food became difficult, too. St Arnaud complained to Raglan that British and French commissaries were bidding against one another for local produce, and one of Raglan's ADCs wrote that 'bread is our greatest difficulty here as it is all sour'.

In the midst of this administrative quagmire, the strategic situation dramatically

changed. During the night of 22/23 June, the Russians raised the siege of Silistria, and by 2 July they had withdrawn completely from Moldavia and Wallachia. However, political and public opinion in London and Paris determined that Russia must be taught a lesson and deterred from ever again threatening the Balkans or the Straits.

A. W. Kinglake, author of a detailed account of the war, would allege that the decision to invade the Crimea was taken by a sleepy Cabinet on 28 June. In reality, the venture had been discussed in political circles since at least December 1853 and widely aired in the press during the three months following. A variety of military figures (including Captain J. R. Drummond RN, who visited Sevastopol in January 1854, and Sir John Burgoyne) had already produced reports and recommendations about the feasibility of such an operation. Cabinet endorsement was a mere formality; Raglan had been warned to prepare for this eventuality before leaving London. The

British commander could not therefore have been entirely surprised when on 16 July he received a dispatch (dated 29 June) from Newcastle: 'The fortress [Sevastopol] must be reduced and the fleet taken or destroyed: nothing but insuperable impediments ... should be allowed to prevent the early decision to undertake these operations.'

Raglan consulted Sir George Brown, not only an experienced soldier but also somebody with whom he had worked closely at the Horse Guards and had wanted as his second-in-command. Brown's response, that they should consider what Wellington ('the great Duke') would have done under the

circumstances, has often been misinterpreted. There were serious military objections to invading the Crimea: it was already late in the year and, once ashore, success would be necessary before the onset of winter; no reliable information was to hand about either the strength (estimates varied between 45,000 and 120,000) or disposition of Russian troops on the peninsula; given the problems encountered during the move to Varna and subsequent time in Bulgaria, rapid agreement between the three allies could not be guaranteed; neither land nor sea transport were readily available; above all, no invasion plan existed. However, Brown recognised that

their political masters were intent on landing in the Crimea and seizing Sevastopol. His observation therefore was not military, but political. Wellington held that officers were constitutionally subject to the wishes of government ministers.

Newcastle's dispatch on 29 June reminded Raglan that he had been forewarned on 10 April, and the Secretary of State later acknowledged that the British commander had obeyed the government, contrary to his own professional judgement. In a separate letter, Newcastle emphasised that 'unless we destroy Russia's Black Sea fleet I do not see my way to a safe and honourable peace'.

Others on the spot expressed their doubts, once the decision to invade the Crimea became known. Burgoyne focused on the proximity to winter, Brigadier-General W. B. Tylden, Raglan's Commanding Engineer, thought it 'a very rash undertaking'; Lieutenant the Hon. Henry Clifford believed the whole idea dangerous in view of its open discussion even before the troops left England: 'The least sanguine look upon the plan as that of a madman and the taking of the place as impossible.' Not much enthusiasm there.

The Adjutant-General of the British Expeditionary Force, Major-General J. B. Estcourt, thought supply and transport still 'very defective ... there is a want of organisation'; and in England *The Daily News* blamed deficiencies on 'our absurd system of throwing aside in peace the machinery we are compelled to make use of in war'. Quite possibly. But an invasion had to be organised. Thus, on 18 July a Council of War decided that steps should be taken to find a landing beach sufficiently large to accommodate the combined force, not dominated by enemy guns and within reasonable distance of Sevastopol.

Three days later, sailing along the west coast of the Crimea in *Fury*, Brown and the French divisional commander Canrobert chose the mouth of the Katcha river, 7 miles (11km) north of Sevastopol. All had not been settled, though. On 28 July, Raglan needed to deal firmly with a French suggestion that the allies stay in Bulgaria to counter any renewed military threat to the Danube and ultimately Constantinople, by pointing to the declared policy of the British and French governments. Then, half-hearted attempts were made to convince the enemy that the objective was Odessa or the Caucasus.

The Russians were not fooled. Even as troops sailed down the Channel from

The armada leaves Varna. Plans to leave Varna and concentrate 15 miles (24km) north in Balchik Bay were disrupted by bad weather. By 9 September, the allied warships, many towing transports full of troops, were strung out across the Black Sea. (Ann Ronan Picture Library)

English ports in February 1854, Field Marshal I. F. Paskevich drew Nicholas I's attention to the bellicose outpourings of the British press about attacking Sevastopol. He believed it likely that an expedition would try to land in the Crimea. On 11 July, Menshikov similarly warned the Tsar of 'an attempt against Sevastopol and the Black Sea fleet'. However, on 12 September the C-in-C West Crimea concluded that it was now too late in the year for such an enterprise. Not his last mistake that year.

Meanwhile, preparations for the allied invasion were slowed down by a major fire in Varna on 10 August which destroyed a vast quantity of stores (including 11,000 pairs of boots) and, perhaps maliciously, was ascribed to Greek saboteurs in Russian pay. Yet more delay occurred

Landing in the Crimea. Despite problems of initial dispersal, the allied armada gathered off Cape Tarkan and on 13 September approached the Crimean coast in good order. After capturing Eupatoria, the following day troops commenced landing in Calamita Bay. (Ann Ronan Picture Library)

through the need to assemble sufficient troop transports, prepare adequate siege equipment and finalise the landing and assault plans. To make matters worse, cholera was still raging. In the first week of August, 8 per cent of the British land force was suffering from it. Nor did the fleet escape: *Britannia* lost 139 from a ship's company of 985. The French, too, were heavily affected, although estimates of 5,000–9,000 deaths were possibly exaggerated. St Arnaud did, however, theatrically observe, 'I am in the midst of a great sepulchre.'

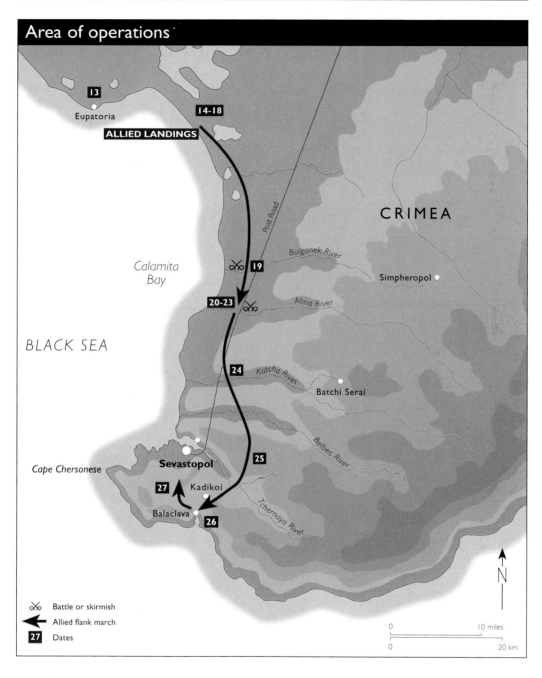

Area of operations

Eupatoria

13

14-18

ALLIED LANDINGS

Post Road

Calamita Bay

Bulganek River

CRIMEA

Simpheropol

19

20-23

Alma River

BLACK SEA

24

Kotcha River

Batchi Serai

Belbec River

Cape Chersonese

Sevastopol

25

27 Kadikoi

Balaclava **26**

Tchernaya River

N

Battle or skirmish

Allied flank march

27 Dates

| 0 | | 10 miles |
| 0 | | 20 km |

At length the cholera abated, and on 20 August final arrangements were made for the troops, horses and equipment to be conveyed either in steam vessels or in sailing ships towed by steamers. Departure would be on 2 September, with embarkation commencing on 24 August. Most of the French and Turkish troops were to be conveyed in their own naval vessels, which could not therefore easily clear for action. However, in view of its inactivity after Sinope, it was assumed that the Russian fleet would not interfere. In Raglan's words, 'the great expedition' was about to begin. Still pointing to the 'terrible' risk so late in the year, the Duke of Cambridge unfairly added, 'but the government insists on it and the commanders have not got the courage to say no'.

Invasion

After embarkation had been completed, the armada aimed to concentrate in Balchik Bay, 15 miles (24km) north of Varna, but 'a strong breeze for several days' disrupted the programme. When Raglan arrived at Balchik on 5 September, St Arnaud had already left. Not until three days later did the two vessels carrying the French and British commanders meet at sea. By then the invasion fleet was strung out over an alarming distance.

That afternoon, an allied conference on board *Ville de France*, St Arnaud's ship, learnt that the French now favoured landing on the south coast of the Crimea at Kaffa, 100 miles (160km) east of Sevastopol and separated from it by mountainous terrain. Reconvened the following day on *Caradoc*, Raglan's steamer, the conference rejected Kaffa, but expressed unease about the proximity of the Katcha to Sevastopol, from which the enemy could quickly bring up troops and artillery.

So on 9 September, protected by three warships, Raglan and 11 British and French officers sailed in *Caradoc* to re-examine the west coast of the Crimea. They returned to the allied ships, which had gathered at the rendezvous 40 miles (64km) west of Cape Tarakan, and announced that the landing area would now be in Calamita Bay, just south of the small port of Eupatoria and 30 miles (48km) north of Sevastopol. Raglan estimated that 20,000–25,000 enemy troops had been seen in camps during the reconnaissance, in addition to the garrison of Sevastopol and others hidden inland at Simpheropol, Batchi Serai and elsewhere.

Skirmish at the Bulganek, 19 September 1854. After allied troops began marching southwards towards Sevastopol, the light cavalry encountered enemy cavalry across the shallow Bulganek river. Massed Russian infantry were then detected in dead ground ahead, and the vanguard extricated from the planned ambush under cover of artillery fire. (Author's collection)

The armada resumed its passage eastwards, and on the evening of 12 September Eupatoria came into sight. Next day it was occupied and the allied force sailed on south to the landing beaches, characterised by the ruins of an old fort. Menshikov received intelligence that the allied armada was at sea while attending the Borodin regiment's ball on 11 September, and confirmation of the impending landings arrived two days later during an evening performance of Gogol's play *The Government Inspector* in Sevastopol. When the news circulated among the audience, the theatre rapidly emptied.

The unopposed invasion commenced on 14 September, but stormy weather interrupted the landings, which were not completed for four days. Then a total of approximately 63,000 men and 128 guns were ashore. St Arnaud wrote confidently: 'The troops are superb ... we shall beat the Russians.' On the morning of 19 September, the march south started: four rivers had to be crossed before reaching the Bay of Sevastopol, which divided the northern suburbs of the naval port from its southern dockyard. The British protected the exposed left flank as the French and Turks advanced adjacent to the coast on the allied right. Two regiments of light cavalry rode ahead of the British force, two covered the flank and a fifth the rear. Cardigan, as brigade commander, went with the two leading regiments, but Lucan had insisted on accompanying the invading force despite absence of the Heavy Brigade and Raglan's reluctance, because the two brothers-in-law had already clashed in Bulgaria.

Reaching the small Bulganek river, which was the first of the water obstacles, during the afternoon of 19 September, Raglan spotted Cossacks beyond. He sent the cavalry advance guard over the stream to investigate. As they did so, the sun flashed on the bayonets of massed infantry drawn up in ambush. Covered by 6pdr and 9pdr field guns, the cavalry skilfully withdrew; and the first skirmish on Crimean territory had taken place.

Battle of the Alma

The march resumed on the morning of 20 September. Kinglake, the chronicler who rode with the army, wrote that it 'was like some remembered day of June in England for the sun was undaunted, and the soft breeze of the morning had lulled to a breath at noontide'. Five days earlier, naval reports had warned Raglan that the Russians were gathering in strength south of the Alma (the second river), which ran into the Black Sea across the allies' front 5 miles (8km) beyond the Bulganek. The ground on its northern (right) bank, across which the Allies must approach, sloped gently towards the river. The south bank, however, rose steeply in places to 15ft (4.5m) and above it 300 to 500ft (90–150m) undulating downs presented an ideal position from which to dominate the river and its approaches. At the extreme western end of the 5.5 miles (9km) of rolling countryside, a 350ft (105m) cliff abutted the Black Sea, where an old Tartar fort overlooked the river-mouth. A ford at the village of Almatamack (a mile [1.6km]) inland and, like Bourliouk and Tarkhanlar, on the north bank) led to a wagon track suitable for artillery; three other paths further east were less accessible.

Three miles (5km) inland, the post road from Eupatoria to Sevastopol passed close to the village of Bourliouk, crossed a wooden bridge and climbed through a gorge overlooked to the east by Kourgane Hill (450ft, 135m), to the west by Telegraph Height. Menshikov discounted any serious attack west of Telegraph Height, identifying the post road as the crucial point. He fortified Kourgane Hill (site of his headquarters) with the so-called Great and Lesser redoubts, respectively armed with 12 and nine cannon. In reality, these 'redoubts' were low breastworks 3–4ft (1–1.2m) high. Nevertheless, the larger one on the lower slopes of the hill, 300yds (275m) from the river, constituted a formidable position. The smaller work faced north-east to deter a flank assault, but could prove troublesome for frontal attackers. The

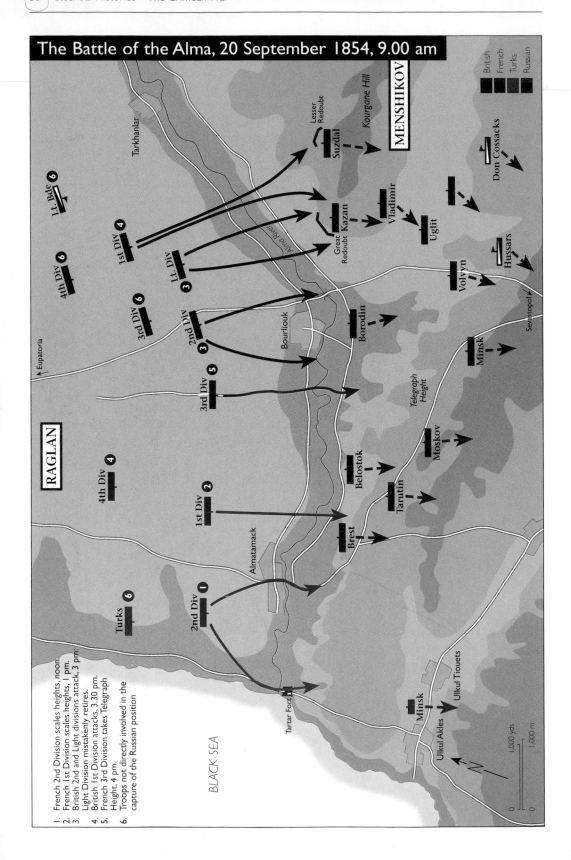

The Battle of the Alma, 20 September 1854, 9.00 am

British
French
Turks
Russian

MENSHIKOV

RAGLAN

Eupatoria

Tarkhanlar

Lesser Redoubt

Kourgane Hill

Suzdal

Don Cossacks

Lt. Bde **6**

1st Div **4**

4th Div **6**

3rd Div **6**

Lt. Div **3**

2nd Div **3**

Vladimir

Kazan

Great Redoubt

Uglit

Volyyn

Hussars

Alma River

Bourliouk

Borodin

Sevastopol

Minsk

3rd Div **5**

Telegraph Height

4th Div **4**

Belostok

Moskov

1st Div **2**

Tarutin

Almatamack

Brest

2nd Div **1**

Turks **6**

Tartar Fort

Minsk

Ulkul Akles

Ulkul Tiouets

BLACK SEA

N

1,000 yds
1,000 m

0
0

1. French 2nd Division scales heights, noon.
2. French 1st Division scales heights, 1 pm.
3. British 2nd and Light divisions attack, 3 pm:
   Light Division mistakenly retires.
4. British 1st Division attacks, 3.30 pm.
5. French 3rd Division takes Telegraph
   Height, 4 pm.
6. Troops not directly involved in the
   capture of the Russian position

third village, Tarkhanlar, 1.25 miles (2km) east of Bourliouk, played no part in the ensuing battle and is omitted from most British maps and accounts.

At the Alma, Menshikov had General P. D. Gorchakov commanding 6 Corps (Lieutenant-General D. A. Kvintsinsky's 16 Infantry Division and Lieutenant-General V. Ia. Kiriakov's 17 Infantry Division) plus one brigade from 14 Infantry Division; a hussar brigade and two Don Cossack regiments of cavalry; four 13 Infantry Division infantry battalions (two from the Belostok and two from the Brest regiments); one rifle battalion; one naval battalion; and one engineer regiment. In all, therefore, he had 42 infantry battalions, 16 squadrons of light cavalry, 11 squadrons of Cossacks and 84 guns. An indeterminate number of patriotic civilian volunteers, hastily enrolled, temporarily swelled the ranks and promptly vanished once the shooting started.

Believing that the steep track on to the heights close to the sea was impassable for military purposes, Menshikov deployed a single battalion of the Minsk regiment with half a battery of field guns near Ulkul Akles, a mile (1.6km) south of the river-mouth. Its purpose was predominantly to warn of undue activity at sea, with one company forward in the Tartar fort to observe allied movement from the north. Menshikov appears not to have ridden over ground himself, but relied on reports from staff officers.

Convinced that the allies could not embarrass him west of Telegraph Height, Menshikov did not position defenders along the Alma until about 2,000yds (1,830m) from the sea, just east of Almatamack. Between there and Telegraph Height (approximately 2,500yds [2,285m]) he placed the four battalions of the Brest and Belostok regiments, with the Tarutin regiment in reserve. Supported by two field batteries of artillery, the Borodin regiment held Telegraph Height, with the Moskov regiment (sent by Khomutov from eastern Crimea) in reserve. These units west of the post road were evidently under Kiriakov, but in retrospect confusion appears to have

occurred over direction of the Borodin regiment, administratively part of Kvitsinsky's 16 Division. An added complication was that Kiriakov was placed under Menshikov's direct command, not that of Gorchakov, his corps commander. Some accounts maintain that Menshikov kept personal control of all the reserves.

Kvitsinsky, still responsible to Gorchakov, exercised tactical command of Kourgane Hill, where he deployed the Kazan regiment in direct support of the two redoubts, holding the Vladimir and Uglit regiments with two Don Cossack field batteries in reserve. Guarding the flank were the Suzdal regiment and two Don Cossack regiments. Astride the post road, 2,000yds (1,830m) south of the Alma, Gorchakov had seven infantry battalions in reserve (the Volyn regiment and three battalions of the Minsk) with a hussar brigade (two regiments) and a light horse battery. Even more cavalry were waiting south of Kourgane Hill.

Vineyards north of the river had been cleared to remove cover for the allies and expose an unhindered field of fire for the Russians. Cavalry patrols scouted towards the Bulganek and riflemen were placed in Almatamack and Bourllouk. Apart from the few dedicated riflemen, the Russians had under 100 rifles to each infantry regiment. Reliance on the short-range, smooth-bore musket meant that artillery had to cover the river crossings. The newly arrived Congreve rockets proved useless because no launcher frames had been sent with them.

Nevertheless, Menshikov had 33,000 infantry, 3,400 cavalry, 2,600 gunners and 116 guns at his disposal and a powerful natural position to defend. Including reserves, approximately 20,000 men and 80 guns were east of Telegraph Height, covering the gorge and Kourgane Hill, the remaining 13,000 men and 36 guns from Telegraph Height to the sea. Menshikov aimed to delay the allies for three weeks to allow time for reinforcements to arrive. Confident of success, he permitted spectators from Sevastopol to take position on Telegraph Height, where hastily abandoned parasols and bonnets were later found. In

Battle of the Alma, 20 September 1854. The entrenched units, supported by field batteries and two redoubts on the dominant Kourgane Hill (centre) covered the post road, faced by the British on the allied left. When the French and Turks failed to make enough progress closer to the sea (beyond right), Lord Raglan launched his men against Kourgane Hill in the face of fierce fire. Artistic licence has increased the height of the hills, which were nevertheless formidable. (Ann Ronan Picture Library)

Sevastopol, Kornilov wrote in his diary: 'The [Alma] position selected by the prince is particularly strong and we are therefore quite content ... God does not abandon the righteous and we therefore await the outcome calmly and with patience.'

On the allied right, 37,000 French and Turkish troops were supported by 68 field guns and the fire of steamers off-shore. The two brigades of Bosquet's 1st Division were separately to use the steep coastal path and that near Alamatamack. To Bosquet's left, Canrobert's 1st Division would scale the heights via other identified tracks, with Napoleon's 3rd Division attacking Telegraph Height frontally. Forey's 4th Division in reserve would back up Napoleon as and when required. Raglan, on the left, nominally had 26,000 men (including 1,000 cavalry) and 60 guns, was out of range of naval gunfire and faced the strongest part of the enemy position.

At about 11.30, the main allied body halted 1.5 miles (2.4km) from the Alma, as Bosquet continued to advance. Naval gunfire in his immediate support commenced at noon. The overall plan provided for Bosquet to climb the heights to engage and distract the enemy, then Canrobert and Prince Napoleon, supported by Forey, would take Telegraph Height. Only after this would Raglan attack Kourgane Hill.

When Bosquet's force approached, the Russian company in the Tartar fort withdrew, and by 1 pm the French were on the heights close to the sea. At almost precisely the same moment, 4.5 miles (7.2km) further inland and still north of the river, the British resumed their advance. After half an hour, they halted again, deployed into line and lay down to await

French success against Telegraph Height. They were now within enemy artillery range. One officer wrote: 'I think the worse part of the whole affair was lying down in lines before we received the order to advance ... The shells bursting over us and blowing men to pieces, arms, legs and brains in all directions.'

An hour and a half later, the French had not taken Telegraph Height because they were unable to get sufficient artillery on to the high ground to support their infantry, as French doctrine required. Far to the allied right, Bosquet was in no position to assist.

Raglan realised, however, that the exposed British were taking heavy casualties on the northern slope, so at 3 pm he ordered his men forward. The Light Division was on the left of the front line, with the 2nd on its right straddling the post road facing Bourliouk village, to which Russian skirmishers had set fire. Behind the Light and 2nd divisions respectively were the 1st and 3rd with the 4th in reserve, as the cavalry guarded the flank.

Having issued his orders, with his staff Raglan crossed the river just west of Bourliouk under the lee of Telegraph Height to a position where he could see clearly both Kourgane Hill and the Russian reserves. Realising that the enemy might be enfiladed from this spot, he sent back for a brigade of the 2nd Division and field artillery to join him. Meanwhile, the Light Division had taken the Great Redoubt ('up the hill we went, step by step, but with a fearful carnage', in the words of one survivor), only for an unidentified staff officer to order withdrawal because he mistook advancing Russian columns for French.

At 3.40, two 9pdr guns reached Raglan and began to harass the enemy on Kourgane

Major-General Sir Colin Campbell (1792–1863).
Led the Highland Brigade at the Battle of the Alma,
commanded the defences around Balaclava, was
directly involved in the 'Thin Red Line' action and
later in the war took charge of the newly formed
Highland Division. (Ann Ronan Picture Library)

As rockets sped the fleeing enemy on their
way, Raglan asked St Arnaud to take up the
pursuit, as he had suffered fewer casualties:
the British lost 362 (including 25 officers)
with another 1,640 wounded or missing. But
the French commander declined, as the
knapsacks of his troops had been left on
the northern bank. The French reported
1,243 casualties (more conservative estimates
thought 63 killed and about 500 wounded,
the larger figure having included cholera
deaths); the Russians incurred
5,511 casualties (including 1,810 dead).

When he heard that the French had
scaled the downs further west, Menshikov
had left Kourgane Hill and fruitlessly ridden
back and forth, unable to decide when or
where to commit his reserves. Returning
eastwards, after the battle had been lost, he
found a distraught, dismounted Gorchakov.
Angrily asked why he was in such a state,
Gorchakov replied: 'I am alone because all

Hill, as the 1st Division in the wake of the
Light crossed the river and retook the
redoubts; the Highland Brigade the Lesser,
the Guards Brigade the Great. Ordering his
command forward, Major-General Sir Colin
Campbell called: 'Now men, the army is
watching us. Make me proud of the
Highland Brigade.' In his detached eyrie,
Raglan observed with admiration: 'Look how
the Guards and the Highlanders advance.'

With Kourgane Hill in British hands, and
the French now on Telegraph Height, at 4.30
the battle was won. Lucan sent the Light
Brigade in pursuit of the fleeing Russians, but
Raglan recalled them. He knew that around
3,000 Russian cavalry had not been
committed to the battle and loss of his own
small force would have vastly hampered
further allied movement. Kiriakov had also
rallied infantry and 30 guns, 2 miles (3.2km)
south of Telegraph Height.

my aides-de-camp and the officers of my Staff have been killed or wounded. I have received six shots.' During a later truce, a Russian officer admitted: 'Yes, gentlemen, you won a brilliant victory at the Alma.'

It was also critical. Failure on 20 September would have brought the Crimean campaign to a premature, ignominious conclusion. However, Menshikov should never have been driven from such a strong position, which he had ample time to prepare. His over-confidence, which encouraged spectators to view the anticipated slaughter, played a major part in the battle's ultimate outcome.

The Flank march. Faced with formidable Russian defences north of Sevastopol Bay, on 25 September 1854 the allies marched round them to the east. The following day, invading troops poured across the Plain of Balaclava on to the Chersonese plateau to besiege Sevastopol. (Author's collection)

Flank march

Possibly because he was terminally ill, but allegedly because his men were fatigued, St Arnaud refused to move on during the following two days. Meanwhile, the dead were buried and Russian wounded evacuated to Odessa. The allied march did not resume until 23 September, to the chagrin of Admiral Lyons, who firmly believed that 'a golden opportunity' had been lost to snatch Sevastopol before the Russians could reorganise. Yet, how Sevastopol was to be attacked had still not been decided: seizure of the northern half then bombardment to induce surrender of the southern dockyard districts; or, alternatively, a march round Sevastopol to the east and a siege of the port from upland to the south. High ground and two more rivers (the Katcha and Belbec) lay ahead, though, before Sevastopol came into sight.

Rear-Admiral Sir Edmund Lyons (1790–1858). Second in command of the Black Sea fleet, in charge of the in-shore squadron and naval liaison officer at Lord Raglan's headquarters; succeeded Vice-Admiral Dundas as C-in-C in January 1855. (Ann Ronan Picture Library)

mouth of the Belbec. Sent ahead to scout, Cardigan reported that an 'impracticable' marsh lay beyond the Belbec, whose causeway was dominated by enemy guns and infantry (Kiriakov's force). That evening a decisive conference took place in camp on the Belbec. The preferred option of taking the northern suburbs preparatory to a bombardment and assault across the bay on the southern dockyard paled. The octagonal Star Fort (its guns capable of 4,000yds [3,660m]) range) had been strengthened by construction of two batteries nearby and support by entrenched infantry. A Polish deserter also claimed that the area had been mined. Sir John Burgoyne 'strongly' favoured marching round Sevastopol to mount a regular siege from the south. The French, worried about the strength of the northern defences, agreed.

Unknown to the allies, Menshikov had made a decision that would fundamentally affect the course of the campaign. On 23 September, he sent Kiriakov with a covering force to the Belbec river, ensured that warships were sunk across the entrance to Sevastopol to prevent penetration by the allied fleets, left a garrison in the port (supplemented by sailors from the sunken ships), marched surplus regiments over the Tchernaya river to the east and began to gather a 30,000-strong field army on high ground beyond. From there, he could threaten the flank of the invaders and keep in touch with reinforcement routes from the north and east.

24 September was a pivotal day for the allies. Intelligence was received that 'yesterday' the Russians had sunk seven warships across the entrance to Sevastopol harbour and built a new earthwork near the

Lieutenant-General Sir John Fox Burgoyne (1782–1871). A distinguished Royal Engineer, before war was declared, he surveyed the defences of Constantinople. In August 1854, he joined Lord Raglan's staff as an adviser. Recalled to London in March 1855. (Ann Ronan Picture Library)

So with Cathcart's 4th Division and the 4th Light Dragoons left at the Belbec to maintain communication with the fleets, the flank march began on 25 September; 'this bold and extraordinary movement, which claims rank with the greatest efforts of military science', according to *The United Service Magazine*. During its course, his escort having temporarily lost its way, Raglan very nearly rode into the rearguard of the Russian field army making its way out of Sevastopol. During the morning of 26 September, the British commander crossed the Tchernaya river and entered the village of Kadikoi 1.5 miles (2.4km) from Balaclava. Approaching the chosen British supply port through a narrow gorge and having been assured of a friendly reception, Raglan was fired on from an old castle at the harbour entrance, which rapidly surrendered.

The choice of Balaclava seemed strange. On the left of the line, the British could legitimately have wheeled on to the upland before Sevastopol and made use of the nearby ports of Kamiesch and Kazatch. But Burgoyne and Lyons urged Raglan to secure Balaclava and the new French commander, Canrobert, agreed. On 25 September, Canrobert had succeeded St Arnaud, who died at sea four days later.

So on 27 September, the allies deployed on the high ground south of Sevastopol with the French on the left and British on the right. The Chersonese upland, shaped rather like a heart, had an eastern escarpment (the Sapoune Ridge) 700ft (210m) high overlooking the Plain of Balaclava. A break in the south-eastern corner (the 'Col') gave access to Balaclava via a steep track. This would be used to transport the British supplies. The boundary between the British and French areas of responsibility was the 'Man of War Harbour', a deep inlet from Sevastopol Bay known to the Russians as South Bay.

The French put their 3rd and 4th divisions under Forey in the siege lines, the 1st and 2nd in a Corps of Observation commanded by Bosquet in reserve behind the British in the south-eastern quarter of

General François Certain Canrobert (1809–95). A divisional commander with the French Expeditionary Force, he succeeded St Arnaud as C-in-C in September 1854. In May 1855 he resigned in favour of General A. J. J. Pélissier, taking over his corps and remaining in the theatre of war. (Ann Ronan Picture Library)

the plateau. The British 3rd and 4th divisions were placed immediately east of the Great Ravine, the southward extension of Man of War Harbour, with the Light Division in its rear. The 2nd Division held the extreme right in the area later known as Mount Inkerman, with the Brigade of Guards from the 1st Division supporting it. The French, therefore, faced the Old Town, containing the artillery and engineer stores; the British, the newer, eastern Karabel suburb with the naval barracks, dry docks and main dockyard area.

At the outbreak of hostilities, the civilian population comprised approximately 38,000 Russians, Armenians, Jews, Tartars and Greeks, many of them traders. The northern Severnaia suburb, across the bay, had industrial buildings and supply depots. Below the Sapoune Ridge, principally with the Highland Brigade of the 1st Division, the British guarded the exposed allied flank against the Russian field army, which also threatened Balaclava across the Plain.

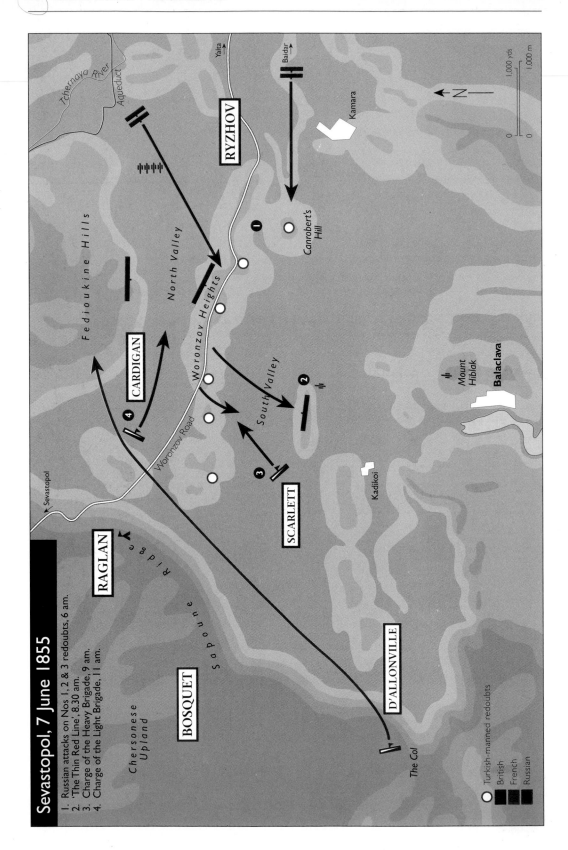

Sevastopol, 7 June 1855

1. Russian attacks on Nos 1, 2 & 3 redoubts, 6 am.
2. 'The Thin Red Line', 8.30 am.
3. Charge of the Heavy Brigade, 9 am.
4. Charge of the Light Brigade, 11 am.

RYZHOV

RAGLAN

BOSQUET

D'ALLONVILLE

SCARLETT

CARDIGAN

Tchernaya River

Aqueduct

Yalta

Baidar

Kamara

Canrobert's Hill

Mount Hiblak

Balaclava

Kadikoi

Fedioukine Hills

North Valley

Woronzov Heights

South Valley

Woronzov Road

Sapoune Ridge

Chersonese Upland

Sevastopol

The Col

1,000 yds

1,000 m

Turkish-manned redoubts

British

French

Russian

The siege opens

As the allies settled on the upland on 27 September, a semicircle of fortifications could be seen facing them, supported by unsunken warships firing long-range from Sevastopol Bay. Apparently, only 23 of the Russian guns on land were effective, but this was not evident to the allies, who believed that 20,000 men were defending the naval port in addition to the field army in the east. In fact, later evidence suggests that, including militia, marines and disembarked sailors but excluding 5,000 workmen, the garrison actually totalled 30,850 men at this time.

Neither Burgoyne nor the French supported an assault without preliminary bombardment, so preparations for one were begun. Answering a request from Raglan, on 2 October Admiral Dundas agreed to land 1,000 marines with a complement of field guns in addition to a naval brigade of 1,040 officers and men with heavier cannon. The Royal Artillery disembarked its siege train, dragging it almost 8 miles (13km) to the heights. The British troops were entrenched 2,300yds (2,100m) away from the enemy, and assaulting across such a wide expanse of open ground would be suicidal without total reduction of the fortifications ahead. On the left, the French put batteries on Mount Rodolph; the British similarly did so on Green Hill and Woronzov Height, 1,300–1,400yds (1,190–1,280m) from Sevastopol, with the Lancaster guns situated in two 'half-sunken batteries' 2,800yds (2,560m) from the enemy. As preparations for the bombardment went ahead, sickness among the troops mounted, and towards the

Gun batteries in action. Heavy mortars and siege artillery fire on the Russians before Sevastopol. The Woronzov metalled road from Yalta is extreme left, the Malakov defence work far right, Sevastopol Bay and harbour entrance in the distance.

Sevastopol from the trenches. The extreme right of the allied line. Note the extent of the naval port and the position of anchored Russian ships, able to fire on to the southern upland. (Author's collection)

end of October Raglan could muster only 16,000 fit men.

What became known as the First Bombardment by 126 British and French guns began at dawn on 17 October. The Russians (now with an estimated 220 guns, including those of steamers in the Bay) forestalled this by opening fire earlier, and there is some suggestion that allied batteries responded prematurely and piecemeal. None the less, the naval 68pdrs in particular proved extremely effective, and Paymaster Henry Dixon of the 7th Royal Fusiliers pleaded to his father that 'you must excuse much as the *row* [sic] is too great to write a line'.

At 10.30, two hits on ammunition magazines silenced the French. Thereafter only 41 British guns were engaged. Moreover, the planned simultaneous naval bombardment did not actually commence until 1.30 pm, achieved little and obliquely proved that the fleets at sea could contribute

nothing tangible to the siege with their guns. On land the British seriously damaged the Malakov and Great Redan works and theoretically opened a way for an infantry assault. But the French were unable to attack the Flagstaff bastion in front of them and Raglan rightly decided that, unless they could do so, his men would be liable to

Vice-Admiral Sir James Whitley Deans Dundas (1785–1862). Commander of the British fleet off the Crimea, which he controlled independent of Lord Raglan. Dundas initially led his warships into the Black Sea in January 1854. With a haughty manner and acutely aware of aristocratic family connections, he was sensitive to perceived slights. (Hulton Getty)

heavy losses from flank fire. The Russians were therefore able to repair their fortifications overnight under the direction of the able engineer Lieutenant-Colonel F. E. I. Todleben.

Although the French did reopen fire the following day and the bombardment continued for a further week, it ended in failure. The Russian commander of Sevastopol, Vice-Admiral Kornilov, was mortally wounded, however, and direction of the military and naval forces devolved separately on Lieutenant-General von Moeller and Vice-Admiral Nachimov.

Battle of Balaclava

Even while the bombardment was in progress, Raglan became concerned about the vulnerability of Balaclava. On 18 September, warned by patrols of movement across the Tchernaya, he rode to the Sapoune Ridge but discerned no immediate danger. Nevertheless, Russian troops had already probed towards the line of redoubts constructed along the Woronzov (or Causeway) Heights, which divided the Plain of Balaclava into two valleys. Further abortive alarms occurred on 20 and 22 October.

Lieutenant-Colonel F. E. I. Todleben (1818–84). Russian engineer responsible for strengthening the defences of Sevastopol, which defied the allies for almost a year. Advised against attacking French and Sardinian troops, which led to Russian failure at the Battle of the Tchernaya in August 1855. (Ann Ronan Picture Library)

river, was 1.5 miles (2.4km) wide, with the Fedioukine Hills on its north side parallel to the Woronzov Heights. The Russian field army lay in the area of Chorgun, north-east across the Tchernaya and due east of the Woronzov Heights beyond Kamara.

Enemy troops could advance over Tractir Bridge and other bridges across the river and the aqueduct, which carried Sevastopol's water supply, at the end of the North Valley to menace six redoubts constructed under Raglan's orders along the Woronzov Heights. These had frustrated Russian patrols so far; but these enemy sorties could be seen from Sapoune Ridge. An attack from distant Kamara was potentially more dangerous and could be detected only by forward pickets.

The redoubts, furthermore, were not quite so strong as expected. Numbered 1–6 east to west, five were spread over 2 miles (3.2km), roughly 500yds (455m) apart, while the sixth (No. 1) was on the detached Canrobert's Hill 1,000yds (915m) south-east of No. 2. Only

Adjacent to Balaclava, to the east, lay Mount Hiblak (dubbed Marine Heights), beyond it the village of Kamara and still further east the Baidar Valley. Kadikoi, through which Raglan rode on 26 September, was 1.5 miles (2.4km) north of Balaclava and across its front at right angles lay South Valley, 4 miles (6.4km) west to east and 1 mile (1.6km) north to south. Dividing the South and North valleys, which comprised the Plain of Balaclava, lay the 300ft-high (90m) Woronzov Heights, along which the metalled Woronzov Road from Yalta ran before climbing the escarpment into Sevastopol. The North Valley, stretching 3 miles (5km) west to east from the Sapoune Ridge to the Tchernaya

The Admiralty Building, Sevastopol, before damage by allied shells. From here Admiral P. S. Nachimov commanded the Russian Black Sea fleet, directed its withdrawal into Sevastopol Bay (background) and the sinking of the naval vessels anchored across the harbour entrance. His Chief of Staff, Vice-Admiral V. A. Kornilov, led the defence of Sevastopol until killed close to the Malakov fortification on 17 October 1854. (Author's collection)

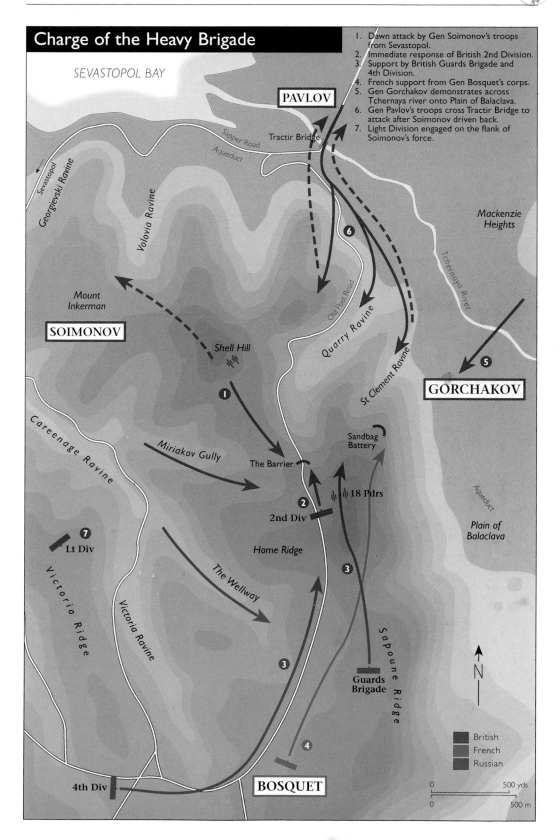

Charge of the Heavy Brigade

1. Dawn attack by Gen Soimonov's troops from Sevastopol.
2. Immediate response of British 2nd Division.
3. Support by British Guards Brigade and 4th Division.
4. French support from Gen Bosquet's corps.
5. Gen Gorchakov demonstrates across Tchernaya river onto Plain of Balaclava.
6. Gen Pavlov's troops cross Tractir Bridge to attack after Soimonov driven back.
7. Light Division engaged on the flank of Soimonov's force.

SEVASTOPOL BAY

PAVLOV

Sapper Road

Aqueduct

Tractir Bridge

Sevastopol

Georgievski Ravine

Volovia Ravine

Mackenzie Heights

Tchernaya River

Old Post Road

Mount Inkerman

SOIMONOV

Shell Hill

Quarry Ravine

St Clement Ravine

GORCHAKOV

Careenage Ravine

Miriakov Gully

The Barrier

Sandbag Battery

Aqueduct

18 Pdrs

2nd Div

Plain of Balaclava

Lt Div

Home Ridge

The Wellway

Victoria Ridge

Victoria Ravine

Sapoune Ridge

N

Guards Brigade

4th Div

BOSQUET

British
French
Russian

0   500 yds
0   500 m

four were armed with 12pdr naval guns; three in No. 1, two each in the next three. On 25 October, Nos 5 and 6 redoubts were unfinished. No. 1 had 600 Turkish militia in and around it; Nos 2–4, approximately 300 each. A British artillery NCO was in charge of each of the four completed redoubts. These 1,500 men with their nine guns formed the outer defences of Balaclava.

Around Kadikoi were six companies of the 93rd (Sutherland) Highlanders, a battalion of Turks and a six-gun field battery. Together with 1,200 Marines on Mount Hiblak and a total of 26 guns, these formed the inner semicircle of defences under Sir Colin Campbell. On the upland above the plain were the five British infantry divisions and Bosquet's French Corps of Observation. Aware of the threat from Kamara, Raglan had posted the Cavalry Division (1,500 sabres)

Charge of the Heavy Brigade, 25 October 1854. As some 2,000 Russian cavalry crested the Woronzov Heights on the brigade's left flank, its commander, Brigadier-General Sir James Scarlett, wheeled to face them and bravely led his squadrons uphill to drive back the enemy, at a cost of 78 British casualties. (Hulton Getty)

below No. 6 redoubt at the western end of the South Valley, 1.5 miles (2.4km) north-west of Kadikoi. Lucan commanded the two brigades, supported by the divisional troop of horse artillery, independent of Campbell but specifically tasked to watch through forward patrols for movement from the Baidar Valley.

Excluding the cavalry, Balaclava's defence force comprised some 4,500 men. Across the Tchernaya, Menshikov had 20,000 infantry, 3,400 cavalry, 2,300 gunners and 78 guns poised to advance via Kadikoi, which he considered the key to Balaclava. Loss of the supply port might persuade the British to abandon the siege.

An hour before dawn on 25 October, the Cavalry Division stood to as Lucan, his staff and Lieutenant-Colonel Lord George Paget, commanding the Light Brigade in Cardigan's absence, cantered eastwards across South Valley. Suddenly flags were seen flying one above the other over No. 1 redoubt – the signal for 'enemy advancing'. Campbell joined Lucan, as an ADC rode back to divisional headquarters, and the two generals decided that a serious situation was developing.

Campbell went towards Kadikoi. Lucan dispatched Captain Charteris to warn Raglan and himself returned to his division. Placing the Light Brigade in reserve, he took the Heavy Brigade eastwards into the valley as a deterrent and sent Captain G. A. Maude's field battery on to the Woronzov Heights close to No. 3 redoubt, because enemy units were reported converging from the north as well as east.

It was all to no avail. At 6 am Nos 2 and 3 redoubts came under artillery and infantry attack, Maude was wounded and his battery soon withdrawn through lack of ammunition. A Turkish battery on Sapoune Ridge and heavy guns near Balaclava lacked the range to unsettle the enemy, whose infantry overran No. 1 redoubt at 7.30. The field battery with Campbell had deployed on the Heights close to Maude's troop of horse artillery, but had to fall back on Kadikoi.

Shortly afterwards, under heavy artillery and infantry attack and outflanked by the loss of No. 1, the defenders of Nos 2–4 redoubts fled, according to Kinglake, crying 'Ship! Ship! Ship!' Near Kadikoi, they were jeered, and in some cases physically beaten, by angry soldiers' wives; Captain C. M. Shakespear observed that 'our sailors kicked their seats of disgrace'. But, in truth, the militiamen were overwhelmed by superior enemy forces. Having dismantled No. 4 redoubt, the Russians concentrated around Nos 1–3, preparatory to cavalry sweeping over South Valley towards Kadikoi and, ultimately, Balaclava.

Warned by Lucan's ADC, soon after 7 am Raglan was on Sapoune Ridge, from which he overlooked the whole plain. Although concerned that the Russians might be practising an elaborate feint to draw troops away from the siege lines, he put the 3rd Division on alert and ordered Cathcart's 4th Division down the Woronzov Road into North Valley, and Cambridge's 1st Division via the Col into the South Valley. Assessing the situation independently, Bosquet sent two French infantry brigades and eight cavalry squadrons down the Col to the western end of South Valley at the foot of the ridge. Raglan, however, became

concerned about the vulnerable position of his Cavalry Division and sent Captain Wetherall with what was later known as the First Order: 'Cavalry to take ground to the left of the second line of redoubts occupied by the Turks'; with Nos 5 and 6 virtually forming a second line, this meant withdrawing west of No. 6.

At 8.30 am the second phase of the Battle of Balaclava began. As 2,300 Russian cavalry supported by 26 field guns advanced westwards along North Valley, four squadrons (400 men) wheeled over the Woronzov Heights close to No. 3 redoubt towards Kadikoi. In the area of a knoll north of the village, they were driven back by 700 British and 1,000 Turkish troops plus Captain G. R. Barker's field battery in an action known as 'The Thin Red Line'. By 9 am the second phase of the battle was over. So far, one phase to each side.

However, the main Russian body was still in the North Valley. Its fate would be decided by Raglan's Second Order, framed to combat the squadrons effectively seen off by Campbell. The British commander sent Captain Hardinge to Lucan: 'Eight squadrons of Heavy Dragoons to be detached towards Balaclava to support the Turks, who are wavering.' By the time that Scarlett and this body was under way, 'The Thin Red Line' had prevailed. Then a greater menace appeared on Scarlett's left flank: almost 2,000 Russian cavalry bearing down in the vicinity of the unoccupied No. 5 redoubt. Calmly turning his regiments to face the enemy, Scarlett led them uphill in two waves, although heavily outnumbered. For some reason the enemy mass halted and, incredibly, the Heavy Brigade drove them back over the Woronzov Heights towards the Tchernaya in confusion. *The Times'* correspondent, W. H. Russell, recorded that 'a cheer burst from every lip – in the enthusiasm officers and men took off their caps and shouted with delight'. In his later dispatch, Raglan referred to the Heavy Brigade Charge (in which a mere 78 casualties were incurred) as 'one of the most successful I ever witnessed'.

There was a bitter postscript. The Light Brigade had sat motionless on Scarlett's left as he charged. Cardigan claimed that Lucan warned him to act only if the enemy attacked; Lucan insisted that he urged him merely to 'be careful of columns or squares of infantry'. Once more the brothers-in-law were at loggerheads, a state of mind which would have even more serious consequences later that morning. It was still only 9.30 am.

Above the plain, Raglan could see the beaten enemy cavalry milling around the far end of North Valley, leaving infantry exposed on the Woronzov Heights and Fedioukine Hills. The enemy was wavering; the time ripe for decisive action. At 10.15 am he sent the Third Order to Lucan: 'Cavalry to advance and take advantage of any opportunity to recover the Heights. They will be supported by the infantry which have been ordered. Advance on two fronts.' Lucan had been in the South Valley all morning: the 'Heights' could only mean the Woronzov Heights, where the Russians were in possession of Nos 1–3 redoubts; 'two fronts' the North and South valleys. Lucan's immediate action suggests that he did understand the order: he moved the Light Brigade into the North Valley, kept the Heavy Brigade in the South Valley and himself took post at the end of the Woronzov Heights between them. But the infantry were delayed and by 10.30 am were not on the plain.

Raglan could see Russian artillerymen preparing to tow away the guns captured in the redoubts. Although spiked, they could be repaired and used against the allies. At about 10.40 am, he therefore dictated the fateful and controversial Fourth Order, which his Quartermaster-General, Richard Airey, copied down: 'Lord Raglan wishes the cavalry to

advance rapidly to the front, and try to prevent the enemy taking away the guns. Troop of horse-artillery may accompany. French cavalry is on your left. Immediate.' As Airey's ADC, Captain L. E. Nolan, left the ridge with the order, Raglan called after him, 'Tell Lord Lucan the cavalry is to attack immediately.' What then happened between Lucan and Nolan will never be known. Undoubtedly, Raglan intended his third and fourth orders to be read in conjunction with one another, the cavalry to move on the redoubts without waiting for the absent infantry. Lucan later maintained that, when questioned by him, Nolan pointed to the

Charge of the Light Brigade, 25 October 1854. Recreated view from the Fedioukine Hills, with Russian troops near the captured redoubts on the Woronzov Heights, centre, Balaclava in the distance. The cavalry lines are too regular. Two regiments (four squadrons) formed the first line, one regiment the second. A further two comprised the third line, but they separated during the charge. (Hulton Getty)

end of the North Valley, where Russian field guns were drawn up to protect the Tchernaya river crossings.

So, shortly after 11 am, Cardigan led 673 men from the Light Brigade plus Nolan, who secured permission to ride with it, up the 1.25-mile-long (2km) valley to be immortalised in Tennyson's epic poem. Twenty minutes later, the shattered remnants returned: 113 men had been killed and 247 badly wounded, 475 horses killed and 42 injured. French cavalry cleared the Fedoukine Hills to protect their right flank as the survivors came back; Lucan was wounded leading the Heavy Brigade to cover

them; Nolan was killed shortly after the brigade commenced its advance. He died in front of Cardigan, waving his sword in the air. Quite what he meant by this action remains in dispute. Perhaps he was trying to redirect the brigade towards the redoubts, as A. W. Kinglake later concluded and countless writers since have repeated.

Scarcely had the last trooper dismounted under the Sapoune Ridge than recriminations started. Raglan censured Cardigan, who pointed to an order from Lucan ('my superior officer'), and the divisional commander laid the blame on Nolan, who could no longer defend himself.

Meanwhile, the two infantry divisions had at length reached the plain, but only exchanged intermittent fire with the Russians during the afternoon. The enemy remained on the Woronzov Heights in possession of the redoubts and the guns were towed away.

However, for all the mistakes and shortcomings of the day, Balaclava had not fallen. Overall, Raglan could claim victory, but few in the Crimea or at home would see the outcome that way; nor would posterity. To most people the Charge was the Battle of Balaclava and that was patently disastrous. Yet in December, the Russians withdrew from the Woronzov Heights. It was as if the battle had never been fought – not, though, for the participants, especially Lucan and Cardigan, for whom it once more stoked the fires of antagonism. In total, the Battle of Balaclava cost the British 480 dead officers and men.

The very next day (26 October) a Russian force moved out of Sevastopol against the British on the right of the siege lines in the skirmish of Little Inkerman. De Lacy Evans's 2nd Division, supported by the Guards Brigade and artillery, successfully drove them off in an action lasting approximately three hours. It cost the British 89 casualties (ten killed), the Russians 350 (including prisoners). Significantly, Bosquet hurried up French reserves in case they were needed – another example of the inter-allied co-operation seen on 25 October.

Battle of Inkerman

This clash was something of a dress rehearsal for a much more serious clash on 5 November. The north-eastern corner of the plateau occupied by the allies before Sevastopol featured an area of high ground about 1.5 by 0.75 miles (2.4 by 1.2km). It was known to the British as Mount Inkerman and the Russians as Cossack Mountain, was bordered on the west by the deep Careenage Ravine, and to the east by the escarpment of Sapoune Ridge. Two gullies (the Mirlakov and Wellway) branched

eastwards from the Careenage Ravine and three ravines (Georgievski, Volovia and Quarry) south of the Sapper Road, which ran parallel to the bay between Tractir Bridge and the port, gave access to the plateau.

Roughly in the middle of Mount Inkerman and 2,000yds (1,830m) south-east of Sevastopol stood Shell Hill, approximately 600ft (180m) above sea level, with two extensions, East and West Gut. About a quarter of a mile (0.4km) from the southern end of the Quarry Ravine, 1,200yds (1,100m) from Shell Hill and 30ft (9m) higher than it, was the L-shaped Home Ridge. This would be the focal point of the forthcoming battle and was where 6,500 'muffin caps' of Russian infantry with four field guns had been repulsed during the skirmish on 26 October.

On Mount Inkerman, which comprised rocky scrubland, were two small defence works. Just north-east of Home Ridge was the Sandbag Battery – an empty 9ft-high (3m) position with embrasures cut for two guns to cover the Tchernaya river below, but no banquette for small arms. In front of Home Ridge, where the old post road emerged from the Quarry Ravine on to the plateau, stood a 4ft-high (1.2m) heap of stones known as The Barrier. Another 2ft-high (0.6m) rampart, called Herbert's Folly, on Home Ridge offered some protection for gunners. There were no entrenchments, only these meagre protective walls.

In this area, the British 2nd Division, commanded by Major-General J. L. Pennefather in place of the sick de Lacy Evans, deployed approximately 3,000 men either south of Home Ridge or thrown forward in pickets. About a mile (1.6km) to the south, the Brigade of Guards was encamped with a troop of horse artillery, but also had a forward picket overlooking the Careenage Ravine. Bosquet's Corps of Observation was yet a further mile south on the upland. The other British divisions were to the west, cut off from Pennefather by a number of ravines; the 3rd, 4th and Light divisions were respectively 3, 2.5 and 1.5 miles (5, 4 and 2.4km) away. Reinforcing

Pennefather in an emergency would not, therefore, be easy.

For Prince A. S. Menshikov, the Russian commander, the episode of Little Inkerman had been no more than a reconnaissance in force. On the basis of what he learnt, he drew up a plan to drive the British from Mount Inkerman and disrupt their communication with Balaclava. General P. D. Gorchakov, with 22,000 troops and 88 guns, would advance across the Tchernaya towards the Fedioukine Hills, 'to support the general attack, distracting the enemy forces … trying to secure the approach to the Sapoune, the dragoons being ready to scale the heights at the first opportunity'. Lieutenant-General F. I. Soimonov, with 19,000 men and 38 guns, was to emerge from Sevastopol at 6 am to cross the Careenage Ravine and advance along the two gullies on to the plateau. Lieutenant-General P. Ia. Pavlov, leading 16,000 men and 96 guns, would leave the Mackenzie Heights at 5 am, descend to the Tchernaya and cross

Tractir Bridge and the aqueduct to attain the heights from the north-east via the three ravines.

These two columns were to meet in the area of Shell Hill at 7 am, where the 4 Corps commander, General P. A. Dannenberg, would take tactical charge of the operation. Lieutenant-General F. F. von Moeller, commanding the land forces in Sevastopol, was to cover the attackers with his batteries and make a demonstration on the allied left to discourage the French from reinforcing Mount Inkerman. The attacking force that was ordered to 'seize and occupy the heights', exclusive of Moeller's troops, therefore totalled 57,000 men and 222 guns, with another 4,000 men and 36 guns in reserve on Mackenzie Heights.

Battle of Inkerman, 5 November 1854. Major-General J. L. Pennefather (mounted centre), temporarily leading the British 2nd Division in place of its sick commander Lieutenant-General Sir Geory de Lacy Evans, watches British infantry repulse Russians (right), as reinforcements approach (left). (Author's collection)

The Battle of Inkerman, 5 November 1854

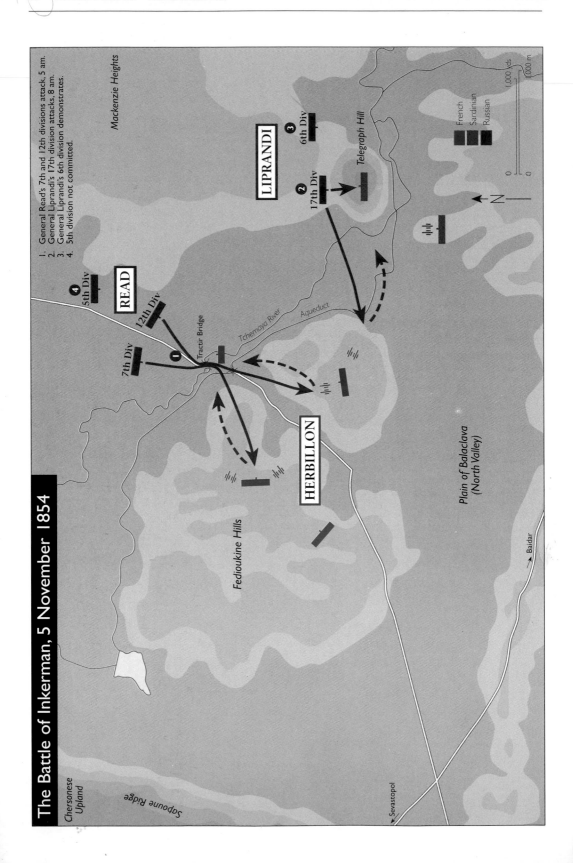

1. General Read's 7th and 12th divisions attack, 5 am.
2. General Liprandi's 17th division attacks, 8 am.
3. General Liprandi's 6th division demonstrates.
4. 5th division not committed.

Mackenzie Heights

LIPRANDI

6th Div ❸

Telegraph Hill

17th Div ❷

READ

5th Div ❹

12th Div

7th Div

❶

Tractir Bridge

Tchernaya River

Aqueduct

HERBILLON

Fedioukine Hills

Plain of Balaclava
(North Valley)

Baidar

Sevastopol

Saponue Ridge

Chersonese Upland

N

French
Sardinian
Russian

1,000 yds
1,000 m

Fortunately for the British, Pavlov and Soimonov did not achieve the required co-ordination, Pavlov being delayed for two hours at the Tchernaya by bridge repairs. Perhaps, even more fortunately, Dannenberg's plan for Soimonov to keep west of Careenage Ravine to clear Victoria Ridge on Pavlov's flank was not followed. Still more galling for the Russians, Gorchakov inexplicably left the bulk of his force east of the Tchernaya, and Bosquet quickly realised that his threat was not dangerous. This allowed the French corps commander readily to support Pennefather.

Heavy rain on 4 November persisted well into the night and at dawn light rain and thick mist still cloaked Mount Inkerman, concealing the Russians' advance. Shortly after daybreak, forward pickets gave warning of their movement, and Raglan reached Home Ridge from his HQ, 4 miles (6.4km) south of Home Ridge, at about 7.30 am. He learnt that Soimonov's troops were making their way on to the plateau, and recognised the threat to the whole Mount Inkerman position. Ordering England's 3rd Division to be vigilant on the British left, he told Cambridge (with the Guards Brigade) and Cathcart (4th Division) to support the 2nd Division. He discovered that Brown had declined Bosquet's offer of help, but promptly welcomed it. Crucially, as it transpired, he feared the range of the Russian artillery, which could reach the British encampments from Shell Hill. Raglan therefore ordered up two 18pdr guns from the siege park.

Soimonov did get 22 12pdr guns on to Shell Hill and West Gut, from which to bombard Home Ridge and the 2nd Division camp beyond. Under cover of their barrage, the Russian infantry advanced south to be met by troops sent forward by Pennefather towards the Sandbag Battery on the right, The Barrier in the centre and Miriakov Gully on the left. As British battalions deployed to meet them, two 9pdr field guns fired over their heads into the gloom. Another six-gun battery went up to the head of the Miriakov, was engulfed by enemy troops debouching

from the gully and lost three guns. A determined counter-attack by the 88th Regiment saved the day and more field guns arrived to raise the number on and around Home Ridge to 36. At the Wellway, the 77th drove back another grey mass; 'no order could be given owing to the fog. All we could do was to charge them when they came in sight,' wrote Lieutenant the Hon. Henry Clifford. By 8 am, Soimonov's infantry were on their way back to Shell Hill. Pavlov had not yet appeared.

When Pavlov's men eventually debouched from the ravines at about 8.30, fierce fighting was renewed, particularly around the Sandbag Battery, which changed hands several times and where French troops were heavily engaged. Not until 11 am was this position finally secure. Seeing bodies piled around the defence work, Bosquet pithily remarked: 'Quel abbatoir!' Meanwhile, as the mist lifted, Raglan had seen that the enemy was close to breaking through between The Barrier and Sandbag Battery, where British troops were fighting desperately at close quarters to protect Home Ridge. Raglan sent word for Cathcart urgently to assist the Brigade of Guards there, but the 4th Division commander decided independently to advance on the extreme right and turn the Russian left. In doing so, tragically he led the troops with him down a gully and paid for the error with his life. His last words allegedly were 'I fear we are in a mess.'

Although the Guards were successfully reinforced, the Home Ridge remained in danger. With Soimonov dead and his division effectively out of the line, Dannenberg had taken command; 9,000 of Pavlov's men were still uncommitted and he now launched them towards The Barrier. Only determined use of bayonet saved the day. One observer recorded that the dead in the area were 'as thick as sheaves in a cornfield'.

At 9.30 am the 18pdrs came into action, while French, British and Russian troops fought bitterly near the Sandbag Battery on the far right. Kinglake later referred to 'the tyranny' of the 18pdrs and Dannenberg acknowledged the 'murderous fire of the enemy artillery'. Undoubtedly, their ability to silence enemy guns on Shell Hill proved important, possibly even decisive. As the Russians streamed away from The Barrier and Sandbag Battery, Raglan sent men to clear Shell Hill to prevent Dannenberg from entrenching on it. Realising that the day was lost, the Russian corps commander ordered a general retreat behind a covering force. By 2.30 pm, the enemy had fallen back from Shell Hill and half an hour later Raglan and Canrobert together watched them recross the Tchernaya in disarray.

The Battle of Inkerman had been won – at a price. Surveying the field of carnage, Captain Temple Godman remarked: 'The field of battle is a terrible sight.' In all,

18pdr guns at Inkerman, 5 November 1854. Sent for by Lord Raglan, two long-range 18pdr guns arrived on the field at 9.30 am, decisively to disrupt the enemy attack. Their protection shown here is too substantial, the visibility less clear on the day. (National Army Museum)

10,729 Russians were killed (including Soimonov), wounded or taken prisoner (a figure rising to 11,974 if casualties from the Sevastopol garrison and Gorchakov's force are added). The British suffered 2,357 casualties, 597 of them killed (including 39 officers, two of them generals). French casualties amounted to 1,743 (175 dead, including 25 officers).

Winter turmoil

In the immediate aftermath of victory, Pennefather exclaimed: 'I tell you, we gave 'em a hell of a towelling.' A cooler appreciation of the allied position was, however, required. A Council of War the following day acknowledged that Sevastopol would not fall before winter. De Lacy Evans was among those who favoured raising the siege and withdrawal from the Crimea.

Raglan realised that this would signal abject failure, successful re-invasion of the peninsula being highly unlikely. He persuaded the doubters that the siege must continue. Frantic requests now went to England for building material to construct 'sheds', more entrenching tools, sandbags, engineers and artillery. In the short term, Dundas agreed to off-load further naval guns and bring up heavy mortars from Malta. Despite the doubts and disputes, the Battle of Inkerman was heralded as another allied victory; and in its wake Raglan became a field marshal.

A 'fearful gale' (to many 'a hurricane') on 14 November swept away tents and equipment and sank 21 British vessels from the Katcha to Sevastopol, including several like *Prince* carrying much-needed supplies. In the words of Corporal W. McMillan, it was 'one of the roughest days that ever man was out in'. Continuing losses of horses and men

through disease and wounds made matters infinitely worse. It was totally unrealistic for a new arrival, Captain Hedley Viccars, to write: 'We are anxiously waiting for Lord Raglan to storm Sebastopol [*sic*]; for, though we must lose many in doing it, yet anything would be better than seeing our soldiers dying there daily.' Raglan did not have enough men to storm the port, and disagreement between the allies over the focal points of the Russian defences did not help either. Burgoyne argued that the Malakov on the allied right was the key fortification; the French, the Flagstaff Bastion west of Man of War Harbour.

So weak was the British situation that Raglan pleaded for not only more men but also urgent replacement of officers: three generals had been killed at Inkerman, three invalided home and three more seriously wounded, numbers that included four divisional commanders (Cathcart,

Scutari Hospital. When Florence Nightingale reached Scutari on 4 November 1854, its two hospitals had a high mortality rate and abysmal hygiene. Miss Nightingale is credited with improving both besides raising the morale of patients. This romanticised scene pays tribute to her work. (Author's collection)

The Great Storm, 14 November 1854. The 'Great Storm' tore down tents, devastated the encampments before Sevastopol and sank 21 ships outside Balaclava harbour (shown here). (Author's collection)

Cambridge, Evans and Brown). Cardigan went home sick to a hero's welcome, while still at the front Lucan erupted in a welter of self-righteousness when Raglan's dispatch on Balaclava became known. In it Raglan criticised the Cavalry Division commander for believing that he must 'attack at all hazards' and further pointed out to Lucan that 'attack' appeared nowhere in the relevant order. The acrimonious dispute between field marshal and lieutenant-general would rumble on until February 1855, when Lucan was recalled by the government to preserve military discipline.

Meanwhile, towards the end of January, the French with their superior numbers had taken over the extreme right of the line in front of the Malakov and Mamelon defence works, while the British concentrated on the Great Redan. At least this solved the strategic problem: the area east of Man of War Harbour was now recognised as the critical point.

Raglan had insufficient men to make adequate roads, and supplies were sadly deficient: 'such roads ... such ground ... such a depth of mud,' Estcourt exclaimed. During the bitterly cold days of December, the fuel ration was reduced and, although more food reached Balaclava, the means to convey it to the siege lines was lacking; the land transport system virtually non-existent. On 14 December, Raglan tersely wrote to Commissary-General William Filder: 'Something must really be done to place the supply of the army upon a more satisfactory footing or the worst consequences may follow.' But Raglan had no direct control over Filder and the Commissariat, even when responsibility for that department passed from the Treasury to the Secretary of State for War ten days later.

Raglan suffered similar frustration with the medical services, which owed allegiance to the Army and Ordnance Medical Department in London. Dr J. (later Sir John) Hall blandly rejected Raglan's complaints about lack of hospital orderlies: 'I considered them sufficient ... and I do still.' Florence Nightingale, who had arrived at Scutari on 4 November 1854 with 38 female nurses due to public and political dismay at reported medical shortcomings, penned a furious letter to Sidney Herbert, Secretary at War in London, about lack of hygiene: 'The vermin might, if they had but "unity of purpose", carry off the four miles of beds on their backs and march with them into the War Office and Horse Guards.' Like Raglan, she was facing the inbuilt inertia and vested interests engrained in a long-standing administrative system. In January 1855, Miss Nightingale gauged that over 50 per cent of the British troops in the Crimea were sick. Captain C. F. Campbell recorded that on one day in that month, the 63rd Foot could parade only seven fit men.

New plans

Plans to renew the siege in earnest quickened in February 1855, especially after the Russians sank six more ships across the entrance to Sevastopol harbour, destroying any hope that they might give up the fight. During the winter's lull in operations, they had strengthened the dominant Malakov defence work and the Mamelon in front of it, now faced by the French on the allied right.

Sickness and casualties, incurred in occasional sorties and exchanges of artillery fire, had reduced the effective British fighting strength to scarcely more than 12,000. Despite this deficiency in men, however, Raglan faced an elaborate French plan to complete the siege of Sevastopol by taking the Star Fort in the north and using 50,000 troops to storm the field army on Mackenzie Heights. Fortunately, the British commander was ignorant of further French proposals to concentrate their reserves at Constantinople. Nor did he know that the Cabinet had needed to reject the idea that British forces should be brought under French control, something attempted by St Arnaud when the allies were in Turkey. In the Crimea, the French now had eight infantry divisions divided into two corps, commanded by Pélissier and Bosquet.

The French plan for the investment of Sevastopol rested to some extent on aggressive action by Omar Pasha from Eupatoria, where on 11 February he commanded 26,000 infantry, two batteries of horse artillery with a third battery about to land. Six days later, the Russians launched a determined assault on Eupatoria, which the Turkish C-in-C drove off. This action did underline the importance of the small port and raise the question of whether the Turks should move against the Russian supply lines from the Perekop peninsula into Sevastopol rather than seek to attack the naval port's northern suburb. An allied strategy was not easy to agree, with all three national commanders now in the Crimea. The French undoubtedly had the largest contingent of troops, but the relationship forged between Raglan and Omar Pasha in Bulgaria endured.

A change of government in London in February 1855, with replacement of Aberdeen and Newcastle as Prime Minister and Secretary of State for War respectively by Palmerston and Panmure, brought an intensification of criticism. Panmure swiftly informed Raglan: 'I see no reason ... to alter the opinion which is universally entertained here of the inefficiency of your general staff.' The Commander-in-Chief at the Horse Guards in London, Lord Hardinge, referred to complaints from 'officers of rank' and *The Times* thundered: 'Their [the troops'] aristocratic generals, and their equally aristocratic staff view this scene of wreck and destruction with a gentleman-like tranquillity ... [they would] return with their horses, their plate and their china, their German cook and several tons' weight of official returns, all in excellent order, and the announcement that the last British soldier was dead.'

Raglan vigorously defended his staff, but Burgoyne had been sent out by the government to be his adviser and was recalled as the ritual scapegoat, leaving the Crimea on 20 March. Without consulting Raglan, the government sent out Lieutenant-General Sir James Simpson as his Chief of Staff 'to inquire into the manner in which the Staff Officers perform their duties' and to ensure that the British commander's orders were quickly carried out. Panmure pleaded: 'I must do something to satisfy the House of Commons.' Meanwhile, Raglan had to fight a war.

In February, too, a Commission of Inquiry went to the front under Dr A. Cumming to investigate the medical services, 'found the patients in the field hospitals generally in a filthy condition' and contrasted the British arrangements unfavourably with those of the French. Palmerston immediately dispatched a more powerful Sanitary Commission of Mr R. Rawlinson, Dr J. Sutherland and Dr H. Gavin, charged with putting not only the field hospitals in the Crimea, but also those at Scutari 'into less unhealthy condition'. This Commission was rapidly followed by Sir John McNeill and Colonel Alexander Tulloch 'to inquire into the whole management of the Commissariat Department'. Although the departments subject to investigation by these various bodies were not under Raglan's command, the impression of incompetence affected perceptions of his inefficiency by those unfamiliar with the tortuous administrative system. On 24 February, Lucan finally left the Crimea in high dudgeon at being recalled, but in truth his continual sniping at Raglan about Balaclava had become intolerable.

As the weather improved in March, the siege lines edged closer to the Sevastopol defences, raising hopes of an early assault. An allied conference on 25 March set 2 April as the date for renewal of the bombardment. According to the Quartermaster-General, Airey, only Raglan's patient 'conferring' persuaded the French to support a combined ground attack in the area of the Mamelon/ Malakov and Great Redan after the bombardment without simultaneous action west of Man of War Harbour. In the event, the long-awaited Second Bombardment by 501 guns (101 of them British) did not occur until 9 April, in poor visibility through mist and rain.

Meanwhile, in March, Nicholas I had died to be succeeded by his son, Alexander II. Menshikov had paid the price for failure at Eupatoria, being replaced by Prince M. D. Gorchakov from Bessarabia. Fearing encirclement south of Sevastopol Bay, Gorchakov soon began surreptitious preparations for withdrawal to the northern suburb across a pontoon bridge of boats.

At a meeting of the three allied commanders on 14 April, Raglan secured agreement to continue the current bombardment less intensely to conserve ammunition, but all decided that a ground assault was out of the question. Shortly afterwards, the full extent of the ambitious French plan for future operations became clear. Having deducted those in hospital and detached on support tasks, Canrobert estimated that the French had 90,000 men available in the Crimea; the British, similarly, 20,000. The Sardinians (formally committed to the alliance in January 1855) had promised to send 15,000 men and Omar Pasha could put 25,000 in the field exclusive of Turks defending Eupatoria. This overall total of 155,000 could be divided into 90,000 to contain Sevastopol and 65,000 to act as a field force. Omar Pasha, however, still favoured an advance from Eupatoria against the northern suburb, and there the matter rested for the moment. The Second Bombardment, in the meantime, petered out with no assault on the defences.

Unknown to the commanders in the Crimea, an even more bizarre plan instigated by Napoleon III had actually been agreed in London. Omar Pasha would continue to hold Eupatoria with 30,000 Turks, as a further 30,000 combined with 30,000 French under Canrobert maintained the siege from the southern upland. Including artillery and cavalry, the 20,000 British would be withdrawn from the siege to join 15,000 Sardinians (who reached the front under General A. La Marmora in May), 5,000 French and 10,000 Turks to form a field army under Raglan. This force would cross the Tchernaya to the Mackenzie Heights. An exclusively French second field army, comprising the 25,000 reserves at Constantinople and 45,000 from the siege of Sevastopol, would concentrate at Aloushita, east of Balaclava, then march northwards to link up with Raglan and complete the investment of Sevastopol.

Neither the logistics of this complicated exercise, nor the mountainous nature of the terrain, seem to have been closely considered. Burgoyne, back in England and present at the relevant meetings, evidently raised no objection. Almost certainly, he calculated that practical difficulties would kill the idea, not least because the number of available Turkish troops had been grossly exaggerated. It also emerged that Napoleon III envisaged taking command of the Aloushita force in person. Then he decided not to journey to the east, and the whole scheme gently faded away. The allies were left to press the siege as best they could. That meant renewed bombardment, followed by an assault on the defences of Sevastopol.

In England, a Parliamentary Select Committee, chaired by J. A. Roebuck, had begun to inquire into the British experiences and became known generally as 'The Sevastopol Committee'. Part of the placebo for political and public angst, which also led to the fall of Aberdeen's government, it concerned itself with Christmas past, provided a platform for the disaffected like Lucan and made no useful contribution to the current position at the front. None the less, news of its proceedings unsettled those conducting operations in the field.

The month of May proved turbulent for the allies. The bombardment was not renewed, though a series of fierce clashes occurred around the siege lines. Omar Pasha threatened to resign because his troops were consigned solely to defensive duties and the Turkish government had agreed to some of his men being placed under Raglan. Canrobert did resign in favour of General A. J. J. Pélissier, remaining in the theatre of war to take over his successor's corps.

A bold change of strategy, dictated by the continued free passage of men and supplies to enemy forces in and around Sevastopol from the east, launched an Anglo-French expedition under Sir George Brown against Kertch at the mouth of the Sea of Azov on 3 May. However, extension of the telegraph to the Crimea had its drawbacks for field commanders. Politicians could quickly interfere with operations, and this was now painfully underlined. After repeated messages

from Paris, the following day the French contingent was ordered back to Sevastopol and the enterprise collapsed.

Fifteen days later, now in command, Pélissier galvanised the French into clearing the Russians from the Fedioukine Hills and all ground west of the Tchernaya, besides making aggressive probes on the upland. He disagreed with grandiose plans for field operations or attacking the northern suburb from Eupatoria. Vigorous pursuit of existing siege operations was the only option. He agreed that the Malakov and Great Redan were the keys to success and that the Mamelon and Quarry positions respectively in front of them must be the preliminary objectives. Furthermore, the Kertch expedition would be remounted.

On 22 May, therefore, Brown once more sailed in command of a combined British, French and Turkish force of 15,000 men, with engineer and light cavalry support. This time the immediate objective was seized plus nearby Yeni Kale, as warships destroyed installations and shipping in the Sea of Azov. Before Sevastopol, fine weather raised morale, horse races and sports' days were organised on the Plain of Balaclava and a lavish Queen's Birthday Parade was staged.

Renewed bombardment

At the beginning of June, the garrison of Sevastopol officially numbered 53,000, including 9,000 naval gunners. On the Mackenzie Heights and in camp at the Belbec were a further 21,000 men and 100 field guns. The allies' Third Bombardment eventually got under way on 6 June and at dawn the following day the French advanced on the Mamelon, while the British assaulted the Quarries. 'It was', according to one observer, 'one of the grandest and most soul stirring sights ever seen,' as both of these objectives were taken and held against determined counter-attacks at a cost of 5,444 French casualties, 671 British (including 47 officers). The higher French losses were explained by a rash, failed attempt to carry on to the Malakov. Despite the undoubted gains, that formidable fortification and the Great Redan still lay ahead. And the French had to some extent been disrupted by a furious dispute between Pélissier and Bosquet, which led to Regnaud de St Jean d'Angely taking over Bosquet's corps on the eve of renewed assault on the Russian defences.

The Fourth Bombardment commenced on 17 June, with 600 allied guns firing along the line from the Quarantine Fort in the west to Point Battery in the east. The shells of 114 French and 166 British cannon fell on the Karabel suburb. After a pause overnight, this aerial onslaught was to recommence at 3 am on 18 June, with infantry attacks going in three hours later. Suddenly Pélissier decided to attack at 3 am without preliminary artillery fire and Raglan had hastily to amend his orders. 'Nothing but confusion and mismanagement' thus prevailed among the allies, in the words of the Hon. Somerset Calthorpe, Raglan's ADC.

The enemy, not for the first time, pre-empted the allies. Then the trail from an enemy shell fuse was mistaken for the executive rocket, and General Mayran on the French right launched his assault prematurely. In the centre and left, generals Brunet and d'Autemarre waited until the agreed signal, so this part of the allied attack went in piecemeal and predictably met fierce resistance. Seeing the French predicament, Raglan sent his men over 400yds (365m) of open ground against the Great Redan without further bombardment. His noble gesture predictably failed, even though a few French and British did temporarily reach the outskirts of Sevastopol. During this action, the British incurred 1,505 casualties, the French 3,500 and the Russians 5,500 (some later Russian accounts claim 3,950). The Malakov and Great Redan, though, remained in Russian hands.

There were, too, wider implications. Captain C. F. Campbell remarked that 'the *entente cordiale* is not at all improved by this disaster'; Paymaster Henry Dixon wrote: 'Everyone seems almost dumbfounded – it is

General Prince Mikhail Dmitrievich Gorchakov (1795–1861). Commander of Russian forces on the Danube, 1853–54, in February 1855 succeeded Prince Menshikov as C-in-C, Western Crimea, to direct resistance to the allies. (Ann Ronan Picture Library)

really the first regular reverse we have had.' The costly setback undoubtedly deeply affected Raglan and may well have contributed to his death on 28 June, when his weak frame succumbed to dysentery. He was succeeded in command by Sir James Simpson, who had come out as his Chief of Staff and quasi government inspector.

The British Expeditionary Force now comprised six infantry divisions (1st, 2nd, 3rd, 4th and Light, with a separate Highland Division) and a Cavalry Division of Light, Hussar and Heavy brigades. With their limited numbers and cholera again prevalent (the French also lost 1,600 men in June), the British were confined to a narrow section of the siege lines overlooking Man of War Harbour and, in co-operation with the Turks, defending Balaclava. The French had the whole of the siege lines west of Man of War Harbour, besides Mount Inkerman and along the Sapoune Ridge.

Mortally wounded in Sevastopol on the day of Raglan's death, 28 June, Vice-Admiral

Nachimov died two days later. During July, the Russian commander, Prince M. D. Gorchakov, came under increasing pressure from Alexander II to attack the allies before their expected reinforcements arrived. The Tsar expressed particular concern at the continuing daily toll of 250 casualties in Sevastopol. On 3 August he wrote of 'the necessity to do something decisive in order to bring this frightful massacre to a close'. Gorchakov prevaricated and called a Council of War. To his dismay, it opted for an assault on the Fedioukine Hills by the field army across the Tchernaya. Todleben, convalescing from wounds, strongly argued against such a venture, which he held had no strategic justification and would not raise the siege. It would be expensive in manpower and utterly pointless.

Battle of the Tchernaya

The Fedioukine Hills lay 1,000yds (915m) from Sapoune Ridge and comprised three separate features scarred by deep ravines, which impeded easy movement. To reach them from the Mackenzie Heights, the Russians needed to cross the Tchernaya, 25ft (8m) wide, 6ft (2m) deep and edged with treacherous marshland, besides negotiating in front of it an aqueduct (canal) with steep masonry sides. Defending the Fedioukine Hills, the French had 18,000 men with 48 guns under General Herbillon deployed each side of the road from Tractir Bridge across the Plain of Balaclava, and they established a bridgehead east of the Tchernaya protected by earthworks.

On the French right flank, some 2,000yds (1,830m) further south and 3,000yds (2,745m) from the escarpment, lay high ground at right angles to the Woronzov Heights, overlooking bridges across the Tchernaya and the aqueduct. This tongue and its vicinity were occupied by 9,000 Sardinians and 36 guns, with an infantry and artillery detachment over the river on Telegraph Hill. A further 50 squadrons of French and British cavalry

were in the area between the Fedioukine Hills and Kadikoi; 20 squadrons of French cavalry, two infantry divisions and 12 guns in the Baidar Valley. Ten thousand Turkish infantry and 36 guns formed additional reserves.

The allies knew that Russians were constructing portable bridges for the river and aqueduct; in turn, Gorchakov was aware that the allies expected an attack. Nevertheless, he was committed to mounting one. On the Russian right, General-Adjutant N. A. Read with two infantry divisions was ordered 'to engage the Fediukin [sic] by artillery fire and prepare to cross the river' in the area of Tractir Bridge, but not to do so without Gorchakov's specific permission. On Read's left, Lieutenant-General P. P. Liprandi, also with two divisions, was similarly to seize Telegraph Hill with one division and await further orders. His second division would move towards Chorgun and the Baidar Valley.

Herbillon, alerted by reports of unusual movement on the Mackenzie Heights during 15 August, was ready when Russian artillery opened up at dawn the following day. Whether Read did so at Gorchakov's behest or independently remains uncertain. But, as part of Liprandi's 6th Division demonstrated towards the Baidar Valley, he sent his troops across Tchernaya under cover of mist shortly after 5 am. Soon they were engaged in bitter close-quarter fighting. Made aware of their predicament, Gorchakov brought up his reserve 5th Division, but like Menshikov at the Alma, he could not make up his mind when or where to commit it. When the mist lifted, the French artillery devastated Read's battalions, as Pélissier ordered forward infantry reinforcements. By 7.30 am, with its commander killed, Read's corps had been chased back over the Tchernaya.

Riding on to the field at about 8 am, Gorchakov ordered eight battalions from Liprandi's force, which had taken Telegraph Hill, to attack north-westwards towards the Fedioukine Hills instead of advancing to their front as planned. In doing so, they were enfiladed by the Sardinians and fell back in confusion. Leaving a rearguard on Telegraph Hill, at 10 am Gorchakov signalled

BLACK SEA

SEVASTOPOL BAY

Careenage Bay

Fort Constantine

Fort Michael

Star Fort

Barracks

Fort Catherine

Sunken ships

Bastion No 1 (Point battery)

Little Redan

Dockyard

Karabel

Malakov

Gervais Battery

Mamelon

Quarries

Great Redan

Barrack Battery

Naval Barracks

Dockyard Creek

Fort Paul

Fort Nicholas

Man of War Harbour

Old Town

Garden Battery

Central Bastion

Flagstaff Bastion

Fort Alexander

Bastion No 7

Quarantine Fort

Quarantine Bastion

Mount Rudolph

French
British

1. Mamelon fortification taken by French, 7 June 1855.
2. Quarries taken by British, 7 June 1855.
3. Malakov fortification unsuccessfully attacked by French, 18 June 1855; taken on 8 September.
4. Little Redan attacked by French on 8 September 1855.
5. Great Redan unsuccessfully attacked by the British on 18 June and 8 September 1855.
6. Attacked by French 8 September 1855.

0   1,000 yds

0   1,000 m

N

Main operations of the Crimean War

Battle of the Tchernaya, 16 August 1855. Russian troops from the Mackenzie Heights (background) cross the Tractir Bridge (centre) and a narrow bridge over the aqueduct (foreground) to be driven back from the Fedioukine Hills by French units including Zouaves. (Author's collection)

a general retreat. The Battle of the Tchernaya (Chernaia Rechka to the Russians) on 16 August had lasted five hours. It cost the French 1,800 casualties; the Russians an estimated 8,000 (2,273 killed); the Sardinians 28 killed.

As Todleben foresaw, the last hurrah of the Russian army during the Crimean War had proved as disastrous as it was fruitless. To Alexander II, Gorchakov blamed the dead Read for not carrying out 'my orders to the letter' – orders that at the time were open to different interpretations and, even in retrospect, remain obscure. Major-General P. V. Veimarn, Read's chief of staff, believed that even if the Fedioukine Hills had been taken, the weight of allied reserves would have prevented any assault on Sapoune Ridge and obliged the Russians to abandon their gains by nightfall. Field Marshal Paskevich concluded that the battle was 'without aim, without calculation,

without necessity and most of all finally eliminated the possibility of attacking anything thereafter' – a damning, but justified, indictment of Gorchakov and his surrender to pressure from Moscow. Four divisions had been used piecemeal; most of Liprandi's force and the reserve division saw no action at all.

Fall of Sevastopol

On 17 August, 704 allied guns opened the Fifth Bombardment on Sevastopol. Lasting four days, it was not, however, followed by the expected renewed assault on the Malakov and Great Redan. That occurred on 8 September after three days of further bombardment (the Sixth) by 775 British and French guns, 57 of them from the Royal Navy, 126 from the Royal Artillery. In the Little Redan, 200 of the 600 defenders became casualties in 12 hours.

West of Man of War Harbour, two French divisions were to attack the Central and Flagstaff bastions, while General M. E. P. M. MacMahon's division stormed the Malakov, Dulac's the Little Redan and that of

The Great Redan. Interior of the earthwork, photographed after the Russian withdrawal, showing its formidable construction and well-placed cannon. (Hulton Getty)

la Motterouge the Curtain Battery. Each of these divisions would be supported by engineers, artillerymen to spike captured guns or turn them on the enemy and, critically, men with scaling ladders. Troops of the British Light and 2nd divisions, commanded by Lieutenant-General Sir William Codrington and Major-General J. Markham respectively, attacking the Great Redan were to be similarly supported and preceded by skirmishers briefed to pick off enemy gunners, making a grand total of 1,900 men. Fears of another débâcle like that of 18 June prevailed, especially as the exposed area short of the objective remained substantially the same. Brigadier-General C. A. Windham, who would distinguish himself on the day, wrote pessimistically to his wife: 'This may possibly, ay and probably will be, the last letter you will ever receive from me.'

Gorchakov believed that the French were waiting for heavy mortars and would not yet attempt an assault. Noon, when the enemy pickets changed, was designated zero hour, but the British and French left were not to attack until a flag signalled capture of the Malakov. Having taken their trenches to within 30yds (27m) of the Malakov, the sudden surge of MacMahon's division caught the Russians by surprise and they were quickly overrun. Cannon in the Curtain Battery, which could have ranged on the Malakov once captured, were spiked, but French troops were driven back from the Little Redan. Pélissier therefore decided to concentrate on holding the Malakov in strength against inevitable counter-attacks. MacMahon told a British officer: 'I'm here, and I shall stay here,' proceeding to beat off the Russians five times.

French troops on the allied left attacked at 2 pm and suffered heavy loss without taking either the Central or Flagstaff bastions. Due to the rocky terrain, the British had been unable to advance their trenches much closer than 400yds (365m) from their

objective, and as on 18 June were enfiladed by withering fire from the Gervais, Barrack and Garden batteries. Although a few brave men (including some from the Naval Brigade) managed to get into the defence-work, they quickly became casualties or were driven out. For the second time an attack on the Great Redan had failed. It cost 2,610 British casualties, 550 of them dead, including 29 officers.

However, as Burgoyne had predicted, the Malakov proved the pivotal fortification. In the final assault on it, the French suffered 7,567 casualties (1,634 killed); Russian casualties were put at 12,000 (3,000 killed). With loss of the Malakov, Gorchakov decided that the southern part of Sevastopol was

Fall of Sevastopol. Following withdrawal of the Russians from southern Sevastopol, fall of the city was greeted with jubilation in England. (Ann Ronan Picture Library)

untenable. During the night of 8/9 September, leaving their wounded behind, the Russians blew up fortifications and important buildings in the port and crossed the prepared pontoon of boats, which they burnt behind them, to the northern suburb.

Next day the allies triumphantly took charge of the dockyard and its environs, claiming that Sevastopol had fallen. But Captain the Hon. Henry Clifford did not rejoice: 'I stood in the Redan more humble, more dejected and with a heavier heart than I have yet felt since I left home … I looked towards the Malakov, there was the French flag, the Tricolour, planted on its parapet … no flag floated on the parapet on which I stood.' He might have reflected, though, that if enemy fire had not been directed at the Great Redan, the French in the Malakov would have been bombarded from batteries not required to engage the British. Thus, on 9 September, the tricolour might not have been flying over the Malakov either. Capture of the main, southern part of Sevastopol with its dockyard and arsenals was truly an allied effort, especially as Turks and Sardinians were in the siege lines.

Windham's fate provides an interesting postscript. Despite his forebodings, he survived the Redan débâcle, became Chief of Staff to the British C-in-C in the Crimea, was later knighted and advanced to the rank of lieutenant-general.

Captain Lewis Edward Nolan

'Attack, sir! Attack what? What guns, sir?' Flinging his arm towards the end of the valley, Captain Nolan replied: 'There is your enemy! There are your guns!' According to Lord Lucan, commanding the Cavalry Division, these comprised the final, fateful words between the two men, which sent the Light Brigade to destruction. But by the time that he recalled them, Lucan had been accused by Lord Raglan of losing the brigade, and having been killed at its outset, Nolan could no longer defend himself.

Early life and career

A slim, dark-haired figure with a trim moustache, Lewis (or Louis) Edward Nolan was an unusual junior officer. He spoke five European languages and several Indian dialects. An outstanding horseman, he had served in a foreign army and published two books about the cavalry, acting as model for their illustrations. He had also designed a cavalry saddle to the satisfaction of the Duke of Cambridge. Born in 1818 in Canada, the second son of an infantry captain, John Babington Nolan, his grandfather, Babington Nolan, had been a light cavalryman. Lewis therefore had a strong military background.

   After returning from Canada and living for a short while in Scotland, the family moved to Milan, then part of the Austrian Empire, where now on half-pay Lewis's father became British vice-consul. At the age of 14, as a cadet Lewis joined the 10th Imperial and Royal Hussars, a Hungarian unit in the Austrian Army, where he was known as Ludwig. Tutored by a renowned riding instructor, Colonel Haas, at the Engineer School near Vienna, he went on to serve with his regiment in the Hungarian and Polish provinces, earning

Captain Lewis Edward Nolan (1818–54). As aide-de-camp to the Quartermaster-General in the Crimea, he carried the fateful order that led to the Charge of the Light Brigade, in which Nolan was killed. (Ann Ronan Picture Library)

official praise for his expert swordsmanship and riding ability. While in England during 1838, he took part in Queen Victoria's coronation celebrations, and the following year he returned to his family in Scotland, ostensibly on sick leave. Nolan never went back to Austrian service.

On 15 March 1839, he purchased a commission in the 15th Light Dragoons of the British Army and sailed with that regiment to India. His stay there was short. In March 1840, he obtained two years' sick leave, though there is no evidence of illness. Back in England, in June 1841 he purchased advancement to lieutenant and in March 1842 was posted to the cavalry depot at Maidstone for a riding master's course. There he impressed Sergeant R. Henderson, an instructor, with his 'thoroughly amiable temper, kindness of disposition and really fascinating manner', besides a transparent devotion to soldiering. Nolan returned to India in May 1843 and the following year became riding master of the 15th Light Dragoons. His 'active and zealous' work brought commendation from an inspecting general. Socially, he was being noted as an accomplished competitor at military race meetings and a conscientious attender at levees, balls and reviews. Appointment as ADC to the Commander-in-Chief in Madras was followed by that of extra ADC to the Governor.

At 31 Nolan had clearly made a name for himself, but he had so far seen no action and would not do so until the Crimea. In March 1850, two months after his father's death, he purchased a captaincy and in January 1851 again secured two years' nominal sick leave. He stayed in Britain a few months before travelling on the continent of Europe to observe cavalry manoeuvres in Russia, Sweden and Prussia. Command of the 15th Light Dragoons' depot troop at Maidstone and of the regiment's detachment at the funeral of the Duke of Wellington followed in 1852. Whilst at Maidstone for the second time, he published his two books: *The Training of Cavalry Remount Horses, A New System* (1852) and *Cavalry: Its History and Tactics* (1853). *The Illustrated London News* proclaimed the latter 'a capital book, written with full knowledge of the subject, both practical and theoretical', and the American Major-General G. B. McClellan praised Nolan's analysis, based on an exhaustive study of military history.

The Crimea

Raglan's ADC and great-nephew, Somerset Calthorpe, considered Nolan 'an officer who, most justly, is very highly thought of by the authorities'. Such was his reputation that he was sent in advance of the Expeditionary Force's arrival in Turkey to buy horses for the cavalry in that country and Syria. He was appointed ADC to Brigadier-General Richard Airey, commanding the first brigade of the Light Division, and went with Airey when he moved to Raglan's headquarters as Quartermaster-General.

The day after the allied armies commenced their advance southwards from the landing beaches in the Crimea, 'the brave and daring Captain Nolan' came under fire during the skirmish on the Bulganek river, reputedly remarking that 'The Russians are damn'd bad shots.' 'The impetuous Nolan,' according to one contemporary, carried messages and orders back and forth during the Battle of the Alma on 20 September. Afterwards, to *The Times'* correspondent W. H. Russell, Nolan angrily denounced Lucan for not sending cavalry after the fleeing Russians.

He accompanied the allied force as it marched round Sevastopol to besiege the naval port from the southern upland. There Nolan continued to decry unimaginative use of the cavalry arm, especially the light cavalry. He considered its traditional role of foraging, pursuing beaten enemy troops after a battle and carrying out reconnaissance forays far too restricting. Years later, Sergeant Henderson recalled: 'I remember, strange as it may appear, that in putting a case hypothetically of cavalry charging in a plain, Captain [then Lieutenant] Nolan drew with a piece of chalk on the wall of the Quartermaster's store in Maidstone barracks a rough sketch which as nearly as possible represented the relative positions of the Russian artillery and the British light cavalry at the Battle of Balaclava; the only thing he was not quite right in was the result. He assumed in such a case the certain capture of the guns.'

Nolan believed that, after the first discharge, the slowness of artillerymen rearming muzzle-loading cannon would allow charging cavalrymen to overrun a battery. Not aware of this, but irritated by Nolan's criticisms in the field, Lord George Paget, Cardigan's second-in-command, observed disparagingly: 'He writes books and was a great man in his own estimation and had already been talking very loud against the cavalry.'

Battle of Balaclava

Throughout the morning of 25 October 1854, Nolan sat above the Plain of Balaclava and saw the inaction of the Light Brigade on the flank of the heavies, when they swept the Russian squadrons back over the Woronzov (Causeway) Heights. His volatile nature and anger at Lucan's perceived incompetence were a dangerous combination, as he plunged down the slope with the decisive Fourth Order. Before he rode off with the message, 'to prevent the enemy taking away the guns', Nolan received 'careful instructions' from Raglan and his immediate superior, Airey. It is inconceivable that either of them briefed him that the brigade was to advance up the valley to attack the Russian guns at its far end. Situated between his two brigades, themselves divided by the Woronzov Heights, Lucan could see neither the redoubts nor the guns at the head of the valley. Hence the reputed sharp scene between him and Nolan.

Having delivered the order, Nolan joined the 17th Lancers and rode with them behind Lord Cardigan, the brigade commander. Before the advance had gone far, he galloped beyond Cardigan, shouting and waving his sword as he looked back towards the brigade. Almost at once he was killed by a shell burst, and his intentions will never be known. It has always been assumed that he suddenly realised Cardigan was moving towards the wrong guns. But, according to Henderson, Nolan thought that light cavalry charging

guns at speed could succeed in carrying them. This leaves the intriguing possibility that, when he died, Nolan was not trying to redirect the Light Brigade, but attempting to get Cardigan, inexperienced in warfare and following the text-book procedure of gradually building up speed, to go faster.

Like the precise content of the exchanges between him and Lucan, the truth can never now be known. Initially, Lucan blamed Nolan for the ensuing débâcle. He may have been right, after all. Perhaps justifiably, therefore, a memorial in Holy Trinity church, Maidstone, would record that Nolan 'fell at the head of the light cavalry brigade in the charge at Balaklava [sic]'.

George Charles Bingham, Lieutenant-General Lord Lucan (1800–88). Commander of the Cavalry Division in the British Expeditionary Force, he misinterpreted Raglan's order and sent the Light Brigade to destruction during the Battle of Balaclava. He vigorously objected to Raglan's criticism of his action and was recalled from the Crimea in February 1855. (Ann Ronan Picture Library)

Women at war

In the first half of the nineteenth century, soldiers and their families were harshly treated. A few blankets slung on a rope across the width of a long barrack-room for flimsy privacy divided the single and married accommodation. There were no quarters outside barracks, nor was special provision made for those left behind once a regiment went on campaign. Six women per regiment were officially then taken on strength to go with the troops. Faced with evidence that up to 30 went with some regiments to Turkey,

Woman in 4th Dragoon Guards Camp. Each regiment was allowed to take six women on strength for duties such as cooking and washing. (Corbis)

but were left to make 'their own way on' from there, the Duke of Newcastle (Secretary of State for War and the Colonies in 1854) 'believed that the soldiers would be dissatisfied if they had not got their assistance for washing and other purposes for which the women generally go with the army'. Although their life would be both onerous and dangerous, the competition to accompany a regiment was keen. Those left behind were likely to endure a squalid existence in penury, reliant on the mercy of unsympathetic poor law commissioners.

Ellen (Nell) Butler

The lot of those chosen to accompany the Expeditionary Force is illustrated by the experiences of a 24-year-old Portsmouth woman, Ellen (Nell), wife of Private Michael Butler of the 95th, who sailed with the regiment from her home port on 7 April 1854. For most of the stormy passage to Turkey, she and the other women were battened below, and Nell burst into tears when allowed freely on deck at their destination. There was little time to rest. Wrapping her scant belongings in a single blanket, she soon joined the march inland, occasionally getting a lift on a bullock cart.

The first night ashore, Nell and her husband unknowingly pitched tent on an ant-hill and woke to discover that most of their rations had been devoured by its occupants. When the armies invaded the Crimea, Nell went on the regimental troopship, but did not immediately land. Unsuccessfully, she tried to spot her husband on the beach through a borrowed telescope. When the sick and wounded began to come on board, the women were again sent below. One night, Nell heard a shout from above to a boat alongside: 'Just send up the live ones, you fool! There were three dead in the last batch.'

At length, she heard that Michael was at Balaclava, sick with fever. Having managed to reach there by steamer, in vain she searched the crowded hospital ships in

harbour, getting more and more desperate: 'The sights I saw there blinded my eyes with tears,' she noted. Suddenly she heard a shout: 'Nurse, come here and hold down this man's hands while I take his leg off.' Despite a flask of brandy, the only available anaesthetic, the wounded soldier remained conscious throughout his ordeal. Nell recalled with horror: 'The doctor took a long bright knife and a saw. I lost feeling and hung on to the man's hands as much to help myself as him. I could hear the grating of the saw.' Understandably, she fainted and was roundly cursed by the doctor when she revived. 'I wasn't able to sew up that artery properly,' he raged, seeking quickly to repair the damage.

Thereafter, she became a nurse by default and thus at length discovered Michael. He would recover enough to rejoin his regiment, but never to regain full strength. Meanwhile, as casualties rose, medical supplies ran short. In her new work, Nell tore up her petticoats for bandages and used old biscuit sacks for poultices. She waxed packthread with a mixture of pitch and fat to prevent it rotting, when surgeons were reduced to using that to repair wounds. During the several bombardments on Sevastopol and attacks against Russian fortifications like the Redan, the ground shook beneath the operating tables. Once a shell landed scarcely 10yds (9m) from Nell, but she went unscathed. However, she did not escape frostbite in her right arm during the bitter winter of 1854–55, and she also suffered from scurvy. When Michael was invalided home with a serious wound, Nell went with him.

They returned to neither a hero's welcome nor financial security. After months of searching, Michael did find a job in Portsmouth Dockyard, but his health gave out and he died prematurely. By now Nell's frostbitten arm had withered, but she gamely took in sewing to supplement the 2s (10p) a week outdoor poor relief. The committee of the national Patriotic Fund, established to assist war widows and families, ruled that 'there is not sufficient evidence to show that Private Butler died from the effects of the Russian War'. Made of stern stuff, Nell did not give up and actively joined others in pressing for justice. At length, Parliament agreed that surviving war widows should receive 5s (25p) a week. When Nell was nearly 80, even that was taken away from her. A month before she died, she wrote: 'I often dream and awake frightened, having seen Michael twice the last month. He was calling me, saying "Nell, Nell, come away or they'll break thy heart".' In 1909, aged 79, she passed away and was buried in her home town with military honours. The coffin bore a brass plate: 'Ellen Butler, Crimean Veteran'.

Frances (Fanny) Duberly

The experiences of another woman who went to the Crimea were quite different. Nell Butler had scribbled her memories in a lined exercise book, later kept in a sideboard drawer. Mrs Frances (Fanny) Duberly kept a detailed journal, which was printed and published. At the age of 20, she married Captain Henry Duberly, ten years her senior and paymaster of the 8th Royal Irish Hussars. A passionate and accomplished horsewoman, Fanny quickly gained popularity with regimental officers as a 'cavalry wife', who followed her husband on campaign at her own expense. Fanny's background therefore differed starkly from that of Nell Butler. The only similarity was that they both went to the Crimea.

With other officers' wives, Fanny set off from Devonport in the sailing ship *Shooting Star* on 25 April. The horses, including Fanny's grey, were held below, each gripped round the belly by a canvas sling secured to the deck above. Placed in two ranks facing one another, wooden mangers were positioned between them. The potential for chaos in choppy conditions clearly existed; and the Bay of Biscay duly produced lashing gales. The vessel's main and mizzen masts were broken, men dodged the frightened hooves of animals as the human sick and injured cried continuously and piteously. Five horses, including Fanny's, were lost

during the stressful voyage. But after a month they reached the Dardanelles in bright sunshine, and spirits climbed.

Fanny recorded that the regiment began to disembark at Scutari prior to occupying nearby barracks on 23 May, but the superficial attraction of colourful accommodation quickly palled on discovery that multitudes of fleas and rats were already in residence. The officers hastily returned to *Shooting Star*. When orders were received to proceed to Varna, the divisional commander (Lord Lucan) forbade any woman to leave Scutari. He had not counted on Fanny's ingenuity. Ostentatiously, she left the ship after persuading two crew members to re-embark her at night. Hidden in the hold, Fanny suffered during repeated delays until at length the ship sailed on 31 May. Then, with Lucan safely ashore at divisional headquarters, she went on deck scornfully to survey the Hotel d'Angleterre where other officers' wives had taken refuge.

She was going to war. The landing at Varna on 1 June proved somewhat disorganised, and the Duberlys' tent was pitched in darkness a mile (1.6km) out of town. Not until 5 June did they leave there on an eight-hour 'jog' to their permanent inland camp at Devna in scorching sun, beset by clouds of dust and flies. To make matters worse, the whole of the Light Division soon arrived, which over-strained food supplies. 'Stale eggs ... and sour milk' became commonplace, to Fanny's disgust. A violent dust-storm on 2 July liberally sprinkled white powder and horse manure over the whole camp. Moreover, Lord Cardigan, the Light Brigade commander, proved a positive pest with a torrent of petty regulations and endless drills. Uncharitably, Fanny hoped he 'will get his head into such a jolly bag that he will never get it out again ... [he] neither feels for man nor horse'. Many men were soon struck down with severe diarrhoea or dysentery, and then cholera began to claim lives.

Moving the whole cavalry camp to another location brought scant relief. There was little opportunity for recreation to

Frances (Fanny) Duberly. An accomplished horsewoman, whose Crimean journal was later published, seen here with her husband Henry, paymaster of the 8th Royal Irish Hussars. (Hulton Getty)

distract her from these problems, though Fanny did make various sketches of her surroundings. On 10 August, she rode 15 miles (24km) to Turkish-held Shumla, a 'picturesquely filthy' town. In the hotel room where she rested, 'the bugs took lease of me and the fleas in innumerable hosts took possession. A bright-eyed little mouse sat demurely in the corner watching me.' Fanny's restful excursion had thus misfired.

En route to Varna, where the Light Brigade would embark for the Crimea, on 29 August she sighted 'the forest of masts, the fluttering ensigns and signal flags' of the invasion fleet. Fanny was forbidden to sail in it. Disguised as a sick soldier's wife she was nevertheless smuggled aboard *Himalaya*, but not until the afternoon of 5 September did the steamer leave harbour. Cholera had meanwhile

struck again and 'faces which should have been bronzed by sun and wind were putty-faced' in terror. Sailing close in-shore on 13 September, even without a telescope Fanny could see a peaceful pastoral scene of houses, cattle and corn on the Crimean peninsula. When the port of Eupatoria surrendered, Fanny explored it on horseback with its new British governor. 'After we had finished our ride, we went to one of the deserted houses, where we found a grand piano – the first I had played on for so long!'

The following day, disembarkation commenced. Like Nell Butler, Fanny Duberly watched from afar. The 8th Hussars did not land until 16 September, when Fanny predicted that Sevastopol would fall 'in a few days'. In the meantime, she went to see her husband, but could only watch from the ship once more as the allied force commenced its southward march on 19 September. That afternoon, Fanny was alarmed to hear distant volleys, unknown to her from the minor clash on the Bulganek river, causing her to worry about Henry's fate. The next day, intermittent sounds of battle on the Alma reached the troopships off Eupatoria, and Fanny's anxiety mounted further. A false report that 'our poor cavalry fellows are all dead' greatly disturbed her. At length, though, reliable information arrived that Henry had survived. Having been thoroughly alarmed, fearing that she might be a widow, Fanny determined never to be parted from her husband again.

Eventually she reached Balaclava, where she stayed on board ship rather than live in a tent ashore. Nevertheless, she made frequent visits to the cavalry camp and the siege lines. One night she stood 'on the brow of a hill … the doomed city [Sevastopol] beneath our feet and the pale moon above; it was indeed a moment worth a hundred years of every day existence'.

On the morning of the Battle of Balaclava, 25 October, a note from Henry warned her that fighting had commenced: 'Lose no time, but come up as quickly as you can; do not wait for breakfast.' Hurrying across the plain, because the Turkish redoubts had already fallen, she reached the heights in time to observe the 'Thin Red Line' clash and the ensuing cavalry charges. As paymaster, Henry did not ride with the Light Brigade during its disastrous charge, but Fanny spent 'a lurid night' recalling the sight of that dreadful spectacle, in which her maid's husband rode to his death.

When supply and transport services broke down before Sevastopol, Fanny bitterly recorded her views of administrative incompetence, which led to widespread suffering among men and horses, besides making Balaclava into 'a village of ruined houses and hovels in the extremest state of all imaginable dirt'. While on board *Sans Pareil* there, she witnessed the devastating storm on 14 November 1854: 'the harbour was seething and covered with foam … I could hardly, even when clinging to the ship, keep my footing on deck.'

However, with the advent of spring and warmer weather, conditions improved. Fanny rode in the 'valley of death', where 'we gathered handfuls of flowers and thought – oh, how sadly – of the flowers of English chivalry that had there been reaped and mown away'. Elsewhere on the plain, troops organised race meetings and Fanny mused that perhaps she should rename her journal 'The Spring Calendar'. After the southern part of Sevastopol had fallen in September, Fanny and Henry explored the ruins of the Redan, where so many lives had been lost, before riding into the port itself. She had a shock. 'We had fancied the town was almost uninjured – so calm, and white, and fair did it look from a distance; but the ruined walls, the riddled roofs, the green cupola of the church, split and splintered to ribands, told a very different tale.'

Fanny Duberly was the only officer's wife to last the entire campaign. Queen Victoria, though, considered her behaviour unladylike, refused dedication of the published journal to her and even ignored Fanny during a review, when one of the royal children pointed her out. Shortly after returning to England, Fanny and Henry left for India. There she was referred to as 'the Crimean heroine', akin to Nell Butler's epitaph. In truth, the two women led far different lives in the Crimea, underlining the social distinctions of the day.

Neither came close to the wretched existence of 250 wives who came out with their husbands but were left in Turkey or Bulgaria when the regiments moved on. Accompanied by their children, some newly born, they were found abandoned in the dark, verminous cellars of the notorious Barrack Hospital at Scutari, many lying 'on a heap of filthy black rags'. Several would be buried anonymously as 'A Woman'.

Guns fall silent

To Queen Victoria, Panmure underlined 'this great success … The excitement is very great.' However, Prince Gorchakov retained a strong force in Sevastopol's northern suburb and his field army still lurked beyond the Tchernaya, totalling, Sir James Simpson estimated, '13 or 14 divisions of infantry, numerous artillery and Cossacks without end'.

Elation swiftly turned to carping criticism, as realisation dawned that the enemy would not soon be crushed. Palmerston complained that 'our two armies seem disposed to rest under their laurels and to live in good brotherhood with the Russians'; the Queen accused Simpson of 'showing a total want of energy of mind'. Panmure expressed his acid displeasure in lengthy dispatches to the British commander, who pointed to the impossibility of assaulting the northern suburb without exposing Balaclava to attack from the Mackenzie Heights. Then he revealed that enemy salvoes across Sevastopol Bay had made southern areas of the city 'untenable', causing withdrawal of allied troops. Evidently, Sevastopol had not been captured after all.

Simpson reacted to Panmure's subsequent angry hectoring by declaring: 'I am mortified and disgusted,' and resigned his command. On 11 November 1855, he handed over to General Sir William Codrington, who reiterated his predecessor's unpalatable assessment: 'The enemy holds as much control over the harbour as we do … it is a large mutual wet ditch under fire from both sides.' In effect, military stalemate. The French, too, almost had a change of C-in-C. Frustrated by lack of forward movement, on several occasions Napoleon III came close to dismissing Pélissier.

Extracted from the ghostly ruins of southern Sevastopol out of range of enemy artillery, at least soldiers on the Chersonese upland enjoyed a more comfortable second winter. Paymaster Dixon explained: 'Our roads are getting on capitally and the railway is splendidly drained, so there is no fear now of our transport breaking down this winter. We also have at least six weeks' stores in advance up here now.' Not least through the influence of Florence Nightingale, medical services improved to the extent that help could be offered to the French.

Kinburn and Kars

Partly to placate the home governments, an allied expedition was mounted to the mouth of the Dnieper river, on the north-western shore of the Black Sea. The British would have preferred to land at Kaffa (Theodosia), on the southern coast of the Crimea east of Balaclava to threaten the enemy field army and interrupt supply lines still in use via the north-eastern Crimea. On 7 October, however, the French prevailed and ten transports carrying 10,000 British and French troops set sail from Kamiesch. They were protected by a powerful naval flotilla of nearly 40 ships, including special boats armed with mortars and three 'floating steam batteries' carrying heavy-calibre siege guns. The immediate objectives were the forts of Kinburn and Ochakov, covering the entrance to the river that led to the naval base at Nikolayev and the provincial capital of Kherson.

After a feint towards Odessa, the expedition anchored close to Kinburn on 14 October. Gunboats then swept a beach 3 miles (5km) upstream on the spit leading to the fort, where, under Brigadier-General the Hon. A. A. Spencer, two British infantry brigades, supported by engineers, artillery and cavalry, landed on the right; French units led by General A.-F. Bazaine on the left. During the morning of 17 October, Kinburn was bombarded from land and sea, at noon the first breach in the walls occurred and three hours later its garrison of 700 surrendered with 80 guns. Next day, the Russians blew up Orchakov and retired northwards. Allied cavalry scouted the hinterland, but it became clear that no further progress could be expected before winter. The main body, therefore, returned to the Crimea, leaving a small garrison in Kinburn to repair damage and prepare for renewed operations in 1856. When the Russians strengthened the approaches to Nikolayev and Kherson, even that force was withdrawn and the pointless military enterprise came to its inglorious close.

Nor was the news from Armenia, where Kars remained under siege, more cheerful. During the summer of 1855, Russian attacks on the beleaguered garrison intensified, but Omar Pasha could persuade neither his own government nor the allies that he should take troops from the Crimea to its aid. Eventually, he left the peninsula on 6 September and a strong contingent of Turkish troops followed him on the 29th. All too late. On 25 November, with food supplies exhausted and disease rife, Kars surrendered. Meanwhile, apart from occasional, ritual exchanges of fire from batteries facing one another across the bay and occasional skirmishes in the Baidar Valley around Sevastopol, 1855 came to an inauspicious close. An enormous explosion in the French lines on 15 November, which killed 80 and wounded almost 300, resulted from mishandling of ammunition not enemy action.

Peace overtures

In the opening weeks of 1856, typhus and cholera struck once more, especially among the French, who suffered over 50,000 cases, of which one-fifth died. Dixon recorded in January: 'The French are dreadfully badly off, much worse than last winter, they are dropping off in scores, nay hundreds.' The British now had an abundance, and in some instances a surplus, of clothing and huts, and as the weather improved they began organising drag hunts and race meetings. Regimental theatres put on plays and a range of speakers delivered educational lectures, too. Militarily, the allies undertook musketry training and field exercises. But it all lacked purpose. In Dixon's words, 'road making here and I suppose diplomacy at home have taken its [fighting's] place'. Soldiers and sailors were marking time until the small print of peace could be fashioned into an acceptable document. French fantasies about attacking Russia's Polish provinces through Germany and British dreams of reducing Kronstadt and Helsignfors (Helsinki) in the Baltic provided the unrealistic backdrop for negotiation.

Almost throughout the entire war, fitful attempts at securing peace had been going on in Vienna, but during the autumn of 1855 clandestine bilateral contacts were also established between Paris and St Petersburg. Discovery of these prompted Austria to take the initiative. On 16 December 1855, Count Esterhazy led a mission to St Petersburg, which conveyed conditions for peace: confirmation of autonomy for Moldavia and Wallachia; freedom of navigation for all nations on the Danube; neutralisation of the Black Sea, with abolition of military installations on its shores; guarantee of the rights of all Christian subjects in Turkey. A fifth condition, allegedly added on British insistence, provided for further matters to be raised during subsequent talks 'in the interest of lasting peace'. The Holy Places in Jerusalem, the Bosphorus and Dardanelles Straits or Sevastopol were not highlighted. In that respect, the Tsar would not be humiliated. However, if Russia did not accept the submission by 18 January, Austria threatened war.

Despite some reluctance and opposition among his ministers, two days before the deadline Alexander II accepted these terms.

Count D. N. Bludov recalled Louis XIV's resignation at the conclusion of the Seven Years War in 1763: 'If we no longer have the means to make war, then let us make peace.' The news reached Sevastopol eight days later. There was still time for forces on both sides to make military points. On 29 January, Russian guns in Sevastopol's northern suburb let loose a vast cannonade against the Karabel and on 4 February the French destroyed Fort Nicholas. Honour seemed to be satisfied. Hostilities petered out.

The peace conference gathered in Paris on 25 February 1856, and three days later an armistice lasting until 31 March was signed. The following morning, 29 February, allied and Russian representatives met near Tractir Bridge to discuss the new situation amicably. Reviews of one another's troops were arranged to celebrate peace, and on 24 March the British commander, Codrington, invited Russian officers to a race meeting near the Tchernaya.

The Treaty of Paris, formally bringing the Crimean War to a close, was signed on 30 March, signalled by a 101-gun salute in the Crimea on 2 April and finally ratified by signatory nations on 27 April. Its provisions referred to 'the independence and territorial integrity of the Ottoman Empire' and the Sultan's 'generous intentions towards the Christian population of his empire … ameliorating their conditions without distinction of religion or race'. The Black Sea was to be neutralised, 'in consequence [of which] His Majesty the Emperor of All the Russias and His Imperial Majesty the Sultan engage not to establish or to maintain upon that coast any military–maritime arsenal'. The principalities of Moldavia and Wallachia were to enjoy 'the privileges and immunities of which they are in possession … under the suzerainty of the Porte … without separate right of interference in their internal affairs … by any of the Guaranteeing Powers'. The principality of Servia would 'preserve its independence and national administration, as well as full liberty of worship, of legislation, of commerce, and of navigation'.

Prince Albert commented: 'It is not such as we could have wished; still, infinitely to be preferred to the prosecution of war.' Queen Victoria consoled herself with the thought that England had saved Europe from 'the arrogance and pretensions of that barbarous power, Russia'. She 'disliked the idea of peace', Lord Clarendon noted, but was 'reconciled' to it. France had no such qualms. The Crimean War was a triumph for

Napoleon III, who had 'given France a glorious victory of arms and peace to Europe'. Russia emerged from the peace talks more buoyant than expected. The naval base of Nikolayev, not being on the Black Sea shore, was excluded from the treaty provisions; shipbuilding had not been banned; although Kars would go back to Turkey, no restrictions were placed on Russian fortifications or troop deployments in the Caucasus; perhaps of most importance, the question of navigation on the Danube was relegated to a series of commissions tasked to report at a later date.

Sightseeing. With an armistice signed, troops crossed one another's lines. Here British officers are depicted sightseeing on the south coast of the Crimea, near Yalta. (Patrick Mercer)

The troops depart

It took some weeks for allied troops to leave the Crimea, Codrington doing so on 12 July with the last of his command. Significantly, before departing, he received the thanks of local Tartars. The third and final commander of the British Expeditionary Force left behind memorials to the battles of Balaclava, Inkerman and the Redan, besides three dedicated to Lord Raglan in and around the farmhouse that had housed his headquarters on the Chersonese upland. By the light of tallow candles and a lantern, provided by their former foes, two British privates completed the blackening of letters on one

of the outside memorials to Raglan at
11 pm on 10 July. Captain Frederic Brine
explained to the Field Marshal's widow that
this 'was the last thing executed by the
British soldier on that blood-stained land'.

Before peace was concluded, 4,273 British
officers and 107,040 men reached the
Crimea, of whom 2,755 were killed in action
and 2,019 died of wounds (4,774 in total).
However, officially 21,097 died in the
theatre of war, which means that 16,323
succumbed to disease, figures that do not
include those who died after returning
home. The French sent out over 300,000
men. French writers give 10,240 killed in
action and a round 20,000 who died of
wounds. Possibly a further 75,000 were lost
to disease. The Sardinians committed 15,000
men, of whom approximately 2,050 died
from all causes. Turkish casualties in the
estimated 35,000 sent to the Crimea are not
clear, but overall allied losses have been
calculated at about 140,000, with the
Russians suffering a minimum 110,000 dead.
The French historian Paul de la Gorce may
not therefore be far wrong in claiming total
losses of over 300,000 among the five
belligerent nations.

Sailing across the Black Sea with the last
British contingent to leave Balaclava,
the adjutant of the Scots Fusilier Guards
issued a stern rebuke: 'There is no objection
to singing in the Officers' Cabin up to
10 o'clock p.m., after which hour it must
cease or Lights will be put out. The singing
last night became a noise and a nuisance.'
They were glad to be going home.

Peace celebrations. At 9.00 pm on 23 April 1856,
following a review by Queen Victoria at Spithead
between Portshead and the Isle of Wight that day,
'the whole fleet at anchor burst into light as by
magic', followed by a spectacular firework display.
(Ann Ronan Picture Library)

Counting the cost

The Crimean War was fought by the allies to remove the threat of Russian aggression against Turkey on land or by sea. Invasion of Moldavia and Wallachia in July 1853 and devastation of the Turkish fleet at Sinope four months later were stark reminders of Russian military potential. Dispute over the rights of Catholic monks in Jerusalem provided an excuse for armed conflict. The more fundamental hidden agenda involved protection of trade routes in the Mediterranean (especially to India), British and French commercial interests in the Ottoman Empire, especially the Levant, and wider stability in south-eastern Europe in the wake of Greek independence and disaffection among Christian subjects of the Sultan.

Neutralisation of the shores of the Black Sea was thus a critical provision in the Peace of Paris. It did not last long. Taking advantage of European preoccupation with the Franco-Prussian War, in 1871 the Tsar unilaterally revoked this clause. Military installations would now be rebuilt and the Black Sea fleet resurrected. The following year Russia agreed to join the Dreikaiserbund with Prussia and Austria-Hungary, which had been devised to isolate France. It also left Britain without support for any action she might wish to take over the Tsar's shredding of the 1856 treaty. Without the political will to enforce its provisions, that document was now worthless. Basically, the land and sea threats to Constantinople and the Straits for which the Crimean War had been fought had been revived. They soon seemed very real indeed.

Balkan unrest

In 1875 and 1876 subject nationalities in the Balkans rose up against their Turkish masters, who responded with customary vigour and cruelty. The 'Bulgarian massacres' caused indignation in London largely through lurid press reports by the *Daily News*. More acutely, they gave Russia an ideal reason yet again to pour into Moldavia and Wallachia and onwards across the Danube to protect fellow Christians. The former British Prime Minister W. E. Gladstone rallied anti-Turkish feeling by calling for the Turks to be cleared 'one and all, bag and baggage … from the province [Bulgaria] they have desolated and profaned'.

However, political and public alarm was heightened when besieged Plevna fell to the Russians, who pressed on to Adrianople in January 1878. Constantinople and the Straits were evidently within the Tsar's grasp. Old fears were reawakened. From merciless villains the Turks were rapidly transformed into wronged victims. Once more Russian ambitions were checked, this time by diplomatic rather than military means through the Congress of Berlin (1878).

But the Russo-Turkish War of 1877–78 and the Bulgarian unrest that preceded it served only to underline the weakness of the Ottoman Empire and re-emphasise that Greek independence (secured in 1830) was likely to be the precursor of political disintegration in the Balkans. And so it proved. By 1913, Turkey would be reduced to a tiny rump west of the Straits, as Romania, Bulgaria, Servia, Montenegro, Albania and Macedonia gained their independence. Unfortunately, the new states could not co-exist peacefully and their quarrels erupted into open warfare in 1912–13. Separation of territories from Turkey, therefore, increased rather than solved inherent problems in south-eastern Europe.

Tragically and directly, in the wake of the Austro-Servian confrontation after the assassination of the Austrian Archduke Franz Ferdinand in Sarajevo, they played a crucial part in the outbreak of the First World War.

Even before that cataclysmic development, the British statesman Lord Salisbury had famously pondered whether during the Crimean War 'we had backed the wrong horse', an effete, corrupt Turkey. Partition of the Ottoman Empire between the major European powers might well have brought elusive stability to the Balkans and Gavrilo Princip therefore might never have fired the fatal shot at the heir to the Austrian throne on 28 June 1914.

Justified war

That having been said, in 1853–54 it would have been difficult not to support Turkey. Russia had been a *bête noire* in the Near East for 30 years, twice in living memory (1828–29 and 1833–41) having threatened either physically to dominate the Straits or politically to force compliance from the Sultan. Since destruction of the Turkish and Egyptian fleets in Navarino Bay (1827) during the Greek war of independence, Turkey had posed no naval threat to the Mediterranean trade routes. Theoretically, Russia did and that was the more immediate consideration. Sinking of Turkish vessels in Sinope harbour with explosive shells, graphically portrayed in the British and French press, provided an added bonus for the bellicose.

In retrospect, Salisbury might have had a point. However, siding with Russia in spring 1854 would have been politically impossible. The cheering crowds that accompanied troops to the railway stations, and others whose handkerchiefs waved them away from the docks, demonstrated the depth of public feeling for the cause. Voices for peace, and others reflecting Charles Greville's view that he had 'hardly seen a madder business', were few and muted. The words of a British soldier, Gunner Whitehead, illustrated the mood of the moment:

Grim War does summon me hence
And I deem it my duty to fight
Tis an honour to stand in proud England's defence
When once she is proved in the right.

Despite question marks about its long-term achievements, the Crimean War did stop Russia from making either political or military progress in Turkey. In 1833 the Tsar had wrung favourable terms out of the Porte in the Treaty of Unkiar Skelessi, which had guaranteed that the Straits would be closed to foreign warships at Russia's request. Nicholas I's instructions in 1853 that his envoy, Prince Menshikov, should hint at occupation of Constantinople and the Dardanelles if negotiations did not go his way, raised the spectre of military action and the possibility of another diplomatic triumph. Allied intervention in the Crimea and the subsequent peace, for all its imperfections, brought these aspirations to a firm halt.

Allied benefits

In Britain, the Crimean War did bring long-term benefit by providing the platform for army reform. In 1854, precisely how many authorities were responsible for the army remained obscure: estimates varied between seven and 14. Small wonder, therefore, that horses starved and men suffered at the hands of an ineffective supply system in the Crimea. There was no Cabinet minister solely in charge of the army. The Secretary of State for War and the Colonies may have had 'authority in all matters relating generally to the army', but the 'colonies' demanded the bulk of his attention, and much of his work fell to another minister, the Secretary at War, whose official duties concerned military law and finance. Military command of the land forces rested with the C-in-C (infantry and cavalry) and Master-General of the Ordnance (artillery and engineers). Supply was the province of the civilian Commissariat (under the Treasury) and Board of Ordnance (responsible to the Master-General).

Schemes for rationalising and improving this ramshackle system had hitherto foundered on lack of support. It had, after all, brought Britain a vast empire during the past 200 years. The furore engendered by press reports of chaos in the Crimea created the political and public atmosphere for change. By 1856, a distinct Secretary of State for War (in fact, the army) had been created and absorbed the responsibilities of the Secretary at War, whose post completely disappeared in 1863. The position of Master-General of the Ordnance vanished; the C-in-C gained command of all the military arms. So one civilian minister and one officer were hence-forth responsible for policy and fighting efficiency.

During the war, glaring examples of supply shortcomings and lack of men for non-military tasks at the front led to five *ad hoc* support services being hastily put together in London and sent to the Crimea. Two survived beyond 1856 to become permanent military bodies. Reports of indiscipline and disorganisation led the Duke of Newcastle, as Secretary of State for War, to create 'a staff corps for the purpose of providing a police force for the army [in the Crimea]'; it was called the Mounted Staff Corps. The Metropolitan Police and Irish Constabulary provided initial recruits, but the corps failed to make an impact and simply faded away. The Civil Engineering Corps, comprising employees under contract hired by a civilian firm, built and maintained the railway from Balaclava to the camps, but did not survive beyond the end of hostilities.

Like the Civil Engineering Corps, the Army Works Corps had been formed for a specific purpose. In May 1855, James Beatty (chief engineer of the railway) wrote: 'That a Civil Corps ... of mechanics, navvies and in fact every description of labourer would be of the greatest service to an army is abundantly shown by the experience of the last nine months here.' The new corps, designed to carry out general labouring work, did not arrive in the Crimea until July 1855. It proved ill disciplined and virtually useless. In the face of protests from politicians that it had been eminently worthwhile, Codrington replied that it would take 'a stretch of imagination' to conclude that the civilian labourers had made any meaningful contribution at the front: 800 were sent home for a range of offences, including persistent drunkenness and insubordination. Codrington suggested to Panmure, Newcastle's successor, that 'your

lordship would be somewhat surprised at the cost ... compared with the real amount of work done'.

Two other of the ancillary corps not only continued beyond 1856, but also became permanent military bodies. The Land Transport Corps, born out of the chaotic inefficiency of the Commissariat's wartime efforts, was reorganised as the Military Train under the C-in-C in London, evolved into the Army Service Corps in 1870 and over a century later merged with other formations into the Royal Logistic Corps. The Medical Staff Corps, to provide hospital orderlies, also owed its birth to the Crimean War. A Parliamentary Select Committee recommended that it 'should continue as part of the Peace Establishment' and in 1857 it was reorganised and renamed the Army Hospital Corps. In 1898 it joined the Medical Staff Corps of doctors to form the Royal Army Medical Corps. Florence Nightingale's work at Scutari and her persistent, post-war pressure for improvements in nursing care in civilian hospitals was another direct result of the Crimean War.

For the Sardinians, siding with the allies brought international recognition, which during the ensuing 15 years played an important role in the struggle to gain a unified, independent state of Italy. In a wider context, the doubtful long-term benefits of the war in political and diplomatic terms were heavily underscored within three years of the Peace of Paris. Yet another serious breakdown of relations between London and Paris led to fear of war with France, the prospect of invasion from across the Channel and formation of the Volunteer Corps to defend Britain's shores.

Nothing, though, could detract from the reform of the British Army, which gave it not only cohesive direction in the hands of one civilian minister and one military officer, but also permanent, military support services. Furthermore, an overhaul of staff training resulted in opening of a dedicated Army Command and Staff College at Camberley in 1862. Without the Crimean War, none of this would have occurred when it did and much of it may never have happened.

Further reading

Calthorpe, S. J. G., *Letters from Headquarters. By an Officer on the Staff*, 2 vols, London, 1856–7.

Fitzherbert, C. (ed.), *Henry Clifford VC: His Letters and Sketches from the Crimea*, London, 1956.

Hibbert, C., *The Destruction of Lord Raglan*, London, 1961.

Kinglake, A. W., *The Invasion of the Crimea*, 8 vols, London, 1863–87.

Russell, W. H., *The Great War with Russia*, London, 1895.

Seaton, A., *The Crimean War: A Russian Chronicle*, London, 1977.

Sweetman, J., *Raglan: From the Peninsula to the Crimea*, London, 1993.

Index

Other titles in the Essential Histories series

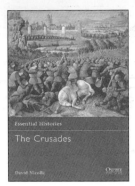

The Crusades

ISBN 1 84176 179 6
February 2001

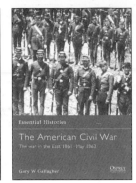

The Crimean War

ISBN 1 84176 186 9
February 2001

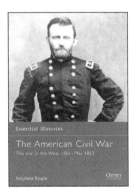

The American Civil War
The war in the East
1861–May 1863

ISBN 1 84176 239 3
February 2001

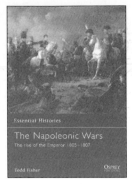

The Napoleonic Wars
The rise of the Emperor
1805–1807

ISBN 1 84176 205 9
February 2001

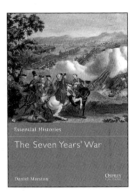

The Seven Years' War

ISBN 1 84176 191 5
July 2001

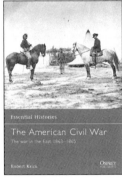

The American Civil War
The war in the East
1863–1865

ISBN 1 84176 241 5
July 2001

The American Civil War
The war in the West
1861–May 1863

ISBN 1 84176 240 7
September 2001

**The French
Revolutionary Wars**

ISBN 1 84176 283 0
September 2001

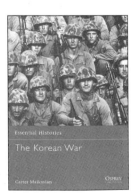

The Korean War

ISBN 1 84176 282 2
September 2001

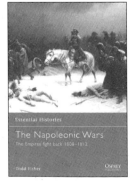

The Napoleonic Wars
The Empires fight back
1808–1812

ISBN 1 84176 298 9
September 2001

The American Civil War
The war in the West
1863–1865

ISBN 1 84176 242 3
November 2001

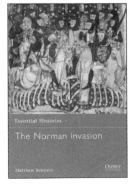

The Norman Invasion

ISBN 1 84176 228 8
November 2001

3/6